Healing the Trauma
of Domestic Violence

A Workbook for Women

EDWARD S. KUBANY, PH.D.
MARI A. McCAIG, MSCP
JANET R. LACONSAY, MA

New Harbinger Publications, Inc.

Publisher's Note

Distributed in Canada by Raincoast Books

Copyright © 2004 by Edward S. Kubany
              New Harbinger Publications, Inc.
              5674 Shattuck Avenue
              Oakland, CA 94609
              www.newharbinger.com

Cover design by Amy Shoup

Cover image: Creatas

Edited by Brady Kahn

Text design by Tracy Marie Carlson

ISBN-13 978-1-57224-369-9

ISBN-10 1-57224-369-4

New Harbinger Publications' website address: www.newharbinger.com

20   19   18

20   19   18   17

Contents

Acknowledgments

We wish to acknowledge all the battered women we have ever worked with. Without their courage to confront their issues and willingness to educate us, this book could never have been written. We also wish to thank the many individuals who read drafts of the chapters and gave us helpful feedback. We especially want to acknowledge Saoirse McCaig, Belinda Kubany, Maile Monroe, and Reb Bellinger for their input and support. We are particularly indebted to Tyler Ralston, who critically read all the chapters and provided a wealth of creative and constructive suggestions.

Introduction

This book was written for you if you are suffering from the aftereffects of having been physically and/or psychologically abused by your husband, boyfriend, or other intimate partner. These aftereffects include symptoms that may continue long after you have left an abusive relationship. Examples of some of these symptoms include

- heart palpitations or breaking into a cold sweat when you see violence on TV

- waking up in a state of panic from dreams of being chased by your abuser

- cleaning obsessively to avoid thinking about the abuse

- not answering the phone because you think it might be your abuser

- not taking pleasure in activities you used to enjoy

- not feeling close to anyone

- not being able to walk down the street without looking around and worrying that you will run into your abuser

- not being able to get more than four or five hours sleep, and not restful sleep at that

- trying to read and finding yourself stuck on the same page for twenty minutes

- yelling at the kids for little things

- feeling guilty that the children witnessed the abuse or are being deprived of their father

- feeling guilty about not having been able to get your partner to change

- feeling guilty about not having broken off the relationship sooner

These aftereffects are quite predictable and often occur as a collection of symptoms called post-traumatic stress disorder, or PTSD.

This book is intended primarily for women who were previously abused by an intimate partner but are now safely out of the relationship. The book may also be helpful for women suffering from post-traumatic stress related to another kind of traumatization—including rape, incest, serious accidents, or the sudden, unexpected death of a loved one.

We are aware that intimate partner abuse can and does occur in same-sex relationships as well as in heterosexual relationships. In fact, we have conducted cognitive trauma therapy with several clients who were abused by a same-sex partner. For ease of communication, however, we always refer to the perpetrator as "he" or "him" and the victim or survivor as "she" or "her."

Finally, this book may also be useful for victim services providers in their work with battered women. The exercises in this workbook can be easily adapted for use in a group format, in support groups, or at shelters for battered women.

What Does It Mean to Say That a Woman Has Been Battered?

A woman is considered to be a battered woman if she was traumatized by physical violence (or threat of violence) and/or psychological abuse by her husband, boyfriend, or other romantic partner. To be *traumatized* means that a person has experienced an intensely negative emotional reaction during a stressful event (American Psychiatric Association 1994). Hence, a woman is a battered woman if she experienced intense fear, helplessness, or horror during violence or abuse by an intimate partner. The intensity of the reaction to the violence is very important because only stressful events that evoke extremely strong negative reactions are likely to produce chronic depression and long-term stress reactions, as in PTSD (American Psychiatric Association 1994).

Most battered women with partner abuse–related PTSD have been traumatized by repeated acts of physical violence. Many of these women have also been traumatized by acts of psychological abuse, including death threats; stalking; sex abuse or coercion to have unwanted types of sex; kidnappings; physical restraint; badgering; harassment or repeated pressure to engage in a variety of unwanted behaviors; verbal cruelty; mistreatment of pets; financial control; property damage; and social isolation.

In fact, some women are traumatized and develop PTSD in response to psychological abuse even if there has been no physical violence in the relationship. In our treatment-outcome study with 125 battered women, 9 women with partner abuse–related PTSD had not been physically abused by their intimate partners but had been terrorized and traumatized in other ways (Kubany et al. 2004). Among these nine women, seven had been threatened with death or serious bodily harm, five had been stalked, and three had been sexually abused by their partners.

Are Men Also Battered?

Unfortunately, many people, including many police officers, think that domestic violence is a mutual kind of thing, where both husbands and wives contribute to the violence and are equally affected or unaffected. And maybe it is mutually reciprocal when most couples fight verbally or where physical aggression is very limited or mild (such as rare instances of pushing, holding, or throwing of objects). But this is not the case in truly abusive relationships, where men purposely use threats, verbal abuse, physical violence, and their strength to control their partners. For example, if the police respond to a complaint of domestic violence and see blood on both the husband and his wife when they arrive at the door, it is *not* the same! The woman may be hysterical and appear out of control (because she is terrified), whereas the man is often calmer (because he is not afraid) and may even appear rational to the police. Unfortunately, the husband's and wife's demeanors may give the police the impression that the woman is the primary aggressor. In fact, women are likely to be terrified and horrified when they are abused by their partners, but men are rarely traumatized when their wives fight back.

Going back to the definition of *battered*, relatively few men are battered because relatively few men experience intense fear, helplessness, or horror in response to physical aggression by their wives or girlfriends. Most men are bigger than their female partners, do not get frightened if their wives or girlfriends become aggressive, and do not feel helpless or out of control, because they know they can stop their partner's violence by physically restraining her or by escalating their aggression toward her. In addition, men are much more likely than women to utilize aggression as a way of dominating and controlling their partner in the relationship. Women are much more likely to utilize aggression to fight back or as a way of defending themselves.

We conducted a study at a substance abuse treatment program which illustrates that men and women do not engage in the same kind of partner aggression and are affected or impacted differently by the aggression (Tremayne and Kubany 1998). Many of the men as well as the women in this program indicated that they had been slapped, punched, or otherwise physically hurt by an intimate partner. However, this is where the similarity ended. Compared to the men,

- women were far more likely to have been threatened with death or serious bodily harm by an intimate partner

- women were far more likely to have been stalked by an intimate partner

- women were far more likely to have been sexually abused by an intimate partner

- women were far more likely to have PTSD than the men.

In addition, other research indicates that male violence against women does much more damage than female violence against men; women are much more likely to be injured by partner aggression than are men (Bureau of Justice Statistics 1995).

Getting Your Wants and Needs Met

Getting personal wants and needs satisfied has not been a high priority for most of our battered woman clients when they start therapy. If you are like most of our new clients, you have been spending most of your time taking care of other people and placing the needs of others above your own. You have probably considered other people's needs more important than your own needs. Similarly, our new clients have tended to place a high priority on anticipating and avoiding disapproval and keeping other people from getting mad or angry. Advocating for their own needs is foreign to many abused women when we first meet them, and many equate self-advocacy or assertiveness with being "rude," "aggressive," "bitchy," or "unfeminine." When our clients stood up for their rights, they often felt selfish and guilty. They were also intimidated by and fearful of interpersonal conflict. One reason for this is that arguments, disagreements, and raised voices are reminders of the abuse; and women with abuse-related PTSD do not like being reminded of the abuse. Much of this workbook focuses on helping you take your power back and establishing you as your own advocate.

Exposing Yourself to Trauma Reminders As an Avenue of Recovery

Avoidance is one of the hallmark symptoms of PTSD. Woman with PTSD will avoid almost anything that reminds them of their abuse (or abuser). However, in order for you to fully recover from PTSD, you need to stop avoiding memories of your abuser or memories of the abuse. While you may not want to think about what happened, facing and reprocessing memories of past abuse is essential if you are to take the emotional charge out of these memories.

While the idea of deliberately exposing yourself to reminders of the abuse and your abuser may seem to be a difficult, if not intimidating, challenge at this point, we think that you can do it, and we will support you if you are willing to give it a try. We will not assign exposure exercises until you get to chapter 14, and by then you may be far better prepared to face your memories than you are right now. If you can get to the place where you no longer become disturbed when you think about what happened and are no longer intimidated by images of your abuser or situations that remind you of him, you will be liberated and empowered.

Most of the women who have completed our program of therapy no longer have PTSD, have had their self-esteem restored, and feel very empowered. They are now able to walk down the street without fear, know what to do if they run into their former abusers, sleep well at night, and are engaging in and enjoying activities they used to enjoy.

Translating a Successful Therapy into a Self-Help Format

Most of the content in this workbook was drawn from an educationally oriented intervention for battered women called cognitive trauma therapy. In fact, the chapters in this book parallel or correspond with various topics covered in cognitive trauma therapy.

Two studies have been conducted to evaluate the effectiveness of cognitive trauma therapy (Kubany, Hill, and Owens 2003; Kubany et al. 2004). Cognitive trauma therapy has resulted in substantial reductions in post-traumatic stress, depression, guilt, and shame, and substantial increases in self-esteem. Because the intervention is based on a learning or educational model, the approach is highly amenable to a self-help format. We believe that many battered women will be able to make significant positive changes in their well-being and quality of life by reading this book, by doing the exercises and homework assignments, and by practicing the recommended self-advocacy strategies on an ongoing basis.

How to Use This Book

This book was not written to be read passively. That's why it's called a *workbook*. We want to actively engage you in an interactive process with us. Critical, rigorous, and logical thinking will facilitate your recovery from PTSD.

The Importance of Writing Out Your Answers

In this workbook, whenever we provide spaces for you to write out your answers, it is extremely important that you put your answers down in writing. The act of responding to the questions by writing your answers in the spaces provided will help you organize and articulate your thoughts and will be helpful in and of itself. Writing your answers is much like writing in a journal or diary, which can help a person clarify her thinking on certain issues and is something she can come back to later and reflect upon. You will get much less out of this book if you do not write down your answers to the questions posed.

We also suggest that you keep a journal while you read this book. When your answers to questions are too long to fit in the spaces provided, we recommend that you write the page number in your journal and expand on your answer in your journal.

Sometimes we ask questions without providing blank spaces for you to write an answer. When we ask you questions this way, we still want you to answer them. It might even help to answer these questions out loud or to write out the answer in your journal.

The Importance of Doing the Homework

In cognitive trauma therapy, we give clients homework to supplement what goes on in the sessions themselves. In this workbook, many of the exercises correspond to the homework assignments in cognitive trauma therapy. To get the most out of this workbook you will need to place a high priority on diligently doing this homework. In the very first session in cognitive trauma therapy, we tell clients that, "What you do between sessions is just as important—and eventually becomes even more important—than what happens during the sessions themselves." Clients who diligently do their homework are far more likely to recover from their PTSD than clients who do not do their homework diligently, on a regular basis.

We strongly encourage you to make every effort to complete all the exercises in this workbook. If you find that you did not complete an assignment, ask yourself, "How can I find a way?" As your advocates on this road to your recovery, we encourage you to focus on looking for ways that problems—such as completing an exercise—can be solved, rather than coming up with reasons why your problems can't be solved. Keep asking yourself, "How can I find a way?"

The Importance of Taking Your Time

In this book, we give you a great deal of information, and there is a lot to absorb and reflect upon. Therefore, we encourage you to only read one chapter per day and to take at least one month to finish the book. Also, many of the assignments are meant to be completed on a daily basis over an extended period of time. For example, the relaxation exercises and the exercise for monitoring the way you talk to yourself are meant to be implemented daily for at least a month.

If you are impatient or get so absorbed in reading this book that you want to read it all in one or two days, that's okay, as long as you go back and reread the chapters one day at a time.

In cognitive trauma therapy, we tape-record all sessions and give our clients audio cassettes of the sessions for what we call "listening homework." Many of our clients find this homework very helpful, and some clients listen to the tapes of their sessions more than once to reinforce what they have learned or to gain additional insights about what they have learned. Many readers of this workbook may find that rereading the chapters (or even rereading them more than once) may also be helpful. Some former cognitive trauma therapy clients have told us that they listened again to the tapes of the sessions much later for therapy "booster shots" or to reflect upon how much they had changed. It might be a good idea for you to reread this book six months or a year from now to reflect upon how you and your life have changed since completing this workbook program.

It may seem to be a daunting challenge, but if you take this program one paragraph at a time, one question at a time, one exercise at a time, and one chapter at a time, the task will be less intimidating than you may think. You have been through a lot, and it may take a while for you to increase your self-confidence and realize that you *do* have the capabilities to overcome obstacles, perform difficult tasks, and make significant changes in your life. If you are like almost all the women who have completed cognitive trauma therapy, you can successfully complete this workbook program.

An Overview of This Workbook

In chapter 1, you will learn about symptoms of PTSD and evaluate whether you may be suffering from PTSD. You will also learn that PTSD is a *normal* reaction to extreme stress and why trauma produces the same kinds of symptoms or reactions in everyone.

In chapter 2, we discuss self-advocacy and how you can empower yourself by becoming your own strongest advocate. In a self-advocacy exercise, we will ask you to evaluate the strength of your beliefs about twenty-five self-advocacy strategies; each of these strategies can empower you and will be important for you to adopt.

Chapter 3 is about anger, which is a common issue for women with PTSD. We discuss several reasons why holding onto anger is not in your best interest and that letting go of anger involves a conscious decision or choice.

In chapter 4, you will learn a technique for monitoring or keeping track of your negative self-talk. To help you become a happier person, we will identify several words and phrases for you to never say or think again. In chapter 5, we will then try to maximize your motivation for breaking negative self-talk habits by providing many reasons why these bad habits drag you down and interfere with your ability to think clearly.

In chapter 6, you will learn about stress, another common symptom of PTSD, and how you can control how you feel by relaxing your muscles.

In chapter 7, you will learn more about PTSD and why thinking and talking about what happened are essential to your full recovery. You will learn that avoiding memories and other reminders of your trauma provide only temporary relief and that behaviors which provide relief are usually not in your best interest.

In chapter 8, you will learn about learned helplessness, which explains why many formerly battered women often feel overwhelmed and believe they are unable to overcome obstacles in their lives. You will learn about the importance of adopting a solution-oriented attitude, which focuses on ways problems can be solved rather than on reasons why they can't be solved.

Chapters 9 and 10 focus on guilt. Trauma survivors tend to exaggerate the importance of their role in trauma and experience guilt that has no logical basis. In chapter 9, you will learn that guilt can be best understood by breaking it apart and examining each of its parts separately. In chapter 10, we will help you get rid of your guilt. We will identify and help you correct numerous thinking errors that have led you to experience guilt.

In chapter 11, we will ask you to critically challenge several "supposed to" beliefs, the kind of beliefs that lead many battered women to stay in an abusive relationship. In chapter 12, you will learn about assertiveness and how to identify disrespectful or aggressive speech in others. You will learn how to get your wants and needs met by being assertive and how to not tolerate disrespect from anyone. Chapter 13 is an extension of the assertiveness chapter. You will learn how to effectively manage stressful and unwanted interactions with former partners.

In chapter 14, we will assign you exercises for exposing yourself to reminders of abuse and your abuser, which will enable you to overcome your fears and to grieve your losses (such as the loss of a marital dream).

In chapter 15, you will learn how to identify potential perpetrators and avoid revictimization. You will learn about numerous red flags that indicate a suitor has the potential to become abusive. Then, you will learn how to determine whether someone is a potential abuser—early in the relationship—when he is charming and may seem too good to be true.

In chapter 16, you will complete the self-advocacy exercise for a second time and see how you have changed since you started this book. If you are like most of the women who have completed cognitive trauma therapy (CTT), you will find that self-advocacy strategies are no longer foreign to you and that advocating is empowering and feels good.

Whom This Book Can Help

This book is for formerly battered women. Many of the things that we teach and recommend women to do could conceivably jeopardize the safety of a woman who is in an abusive relationship. For example, we recommend that women make getting their own wants and needs satisfied a top priority. We advocate that they not tolerate disrespect. This kind of self-advocacy could be potentially dangerous in an abusive relationship. On the other hand, assertive and self-advocacy strategies are good for women who are out of abusive relationships or may be in the early stages of a relationship with a new man. Such strategies can help you avoid ever being victimized again.

It would be difficult, if not impossible, to eliminate PTSD in a woman who is in an ongoing abusive relationship, even if the abuse only occurs once in a while. People do not get over PTSD if the threat of retraumatization looms or if retraumatization occurs. We will illustrate with an example of combat trauma. Let's say a soldier was traumatized and developed PTSD after his unit was ambushed and several of his buddies killed. Let's say we pull him off the front lines, provide him with rest and recreation, treat his post-traumatic stress, and then send him on another combat mission, in which more people in the unit get killed. Do you think his PTSD will go away or not come back? Not very likely! If trauma or the threat of trauma is ongoing, it may be extremely difficult to help someone get over their PTSD; it may not even be adaptive to recover. It may be more adaptive to remain emotionally shut down in order to reduce the emotional impact of subsequent trauma than to open up and experience the full emotional hurt of subsequent trauma.

A cautionary note: Our intervention research has focused on women who are no longer in an abusive relationship and are relatively safe. This workbook is based on that research. If you try to implement our strategies while you are in a relationship with an abusive or potentially abusive person, it is extremely important that you be in contact with a victim services provider and have a safety plan.

CHAPTER 1

What Is PTSD and Do You Have It?

Women who have been physically or emotionally abused by their husbands, boyfriends, or other intimate partners often experience symptoms of post-traumatic stress disorder (PTSD). PTSD symptoms are normal reactions to extreme stress. You are having these problems because of what happened to you—not because of anything about you.

PTSD Questionnaire

We are going to ask you questions about twenty PTSD symptoms to determine if you have PTSD. Answer each question yes or no, and for each yes answer give a brief example or describe a situation in which you had this symptom. Write your answers in the spaces provided. If you need more space, you can write in your journal.

1. Do you have unwanted thoughts or mental pictures about the abuse when nothing is happening to remind you?   Yes ____   No ____

2. Do you have distressing dreams or nightmares about the abuse?
Yes _____ No _____

_____

3. Do you suddenly relive or have flashbacks of the abuse or act or feel as if the abuse is actually happening again?   Yes _____ No _____

_____

4. Do you get distressed or emotionally upset when reminded of the abuse?
Yes _____ No _____

_____

5. Do you have physical reactions when reminded of the abuse? For example, do your palms sweat? Do you breathe rapidly? Does your heart pound? Does your mouth get dry? Do your muscles get tense? Do you have a nervous stomach?
Yes _____ No _____

_____

6. Do you try to avoid thoughts or feelings that will remind you of the abuse?
Yes _____ No _____

_____

7. Do you try to avoid activities, conversations, people, or places that will remind you of the abuse?   Yes _____ No _____

_____

8. Are you unable to remember some important part(s) of the abuse or events related to the abuse in some way?   Yes _____ No _____

_____

9. Have you lost of interest in important activities, such as your job, hobbies, sports, or social activities?   Yes _____ No _____

_____

10. Do you feel detached or cut off from others around you?   Yes _____ No _____

_____

11. Do you feel emotionally numb? For example, are you unable to experience loving feelings, joyful feelings, happy feelings? Or are you unable to cry?
Yes _____ No _____

_____

12. Do you think your future will be cut short in some way? For example, do you doubt whether you will have a career, marriage, or children, or do you expect a shortened life or think you will die prematurely?   Yes _____ No _____

13. Do you have difficulty falling or staying asleep?   Yes _____ No _____

14. Are you irritable or angry?   Yes _____ No _____

15. Do you have trouble concentrating?   Yes _____ No _____

16. Are you hyperalert, watchful, or on guard? For example, do you often look around you to check who might be there? Do you often check to see if windows and doors are locked?   Yes _____ No _____

17. Are you jumpy or are you startled by sudden sounds or movements? Yes _____   No _____

18. Do you experience guilt that is related to the abuse in some way? In other words, do you get upset because you think you should have thought, felt, or acted differently?   Yes _____ No _____

19. Do you experience anger that is related to the abuse in some way? In other words, do you get upset because you think someone else should have thought, felt, or acted differently?   Yes _____ No _____

20. Do you experience grief, sorrow, or feelings of loss that are related to the abuse in some way?   Yes _____ No _____

All of the above are symptoms of post-traumatic stress disorder. PTSD is a collection or set of problems that tend to cluster or occur together as a syndrome—just like the flu is characterized by a collection of symptoms that occur together. The *Diagnostic and Statistical Manual of Mental Disorders* (American Psychiatric Association 1994), hereafter referred to as *DSM-IV*, specifies three primary PTSD symptom clusters. If you look at the list of questions you just answered, questions 1 to 5 refer to the *reexperiencing* symptom cluster. Questions 6 to 12 refer to the *numbing* and *avoidance* symptom cluster. And questions 13 to 17 refer to the *hyperarousal* symptom cluster. A person has to have symptoms from each of these clusters to receive a diagnosis of PTSD. More specifically, to have PTSD, a person must have at least one reexperiencing symptom, at least three numbing or avoidance symptoms, and at least two hyperarousal symptoms.

Estimating Whether You Have PTSD

To determine if you have PTSD

1. Write your number of yes answers to questions 1 to 5: _____

2. Write your number of yes answers to questions 6 to 12: _____

3. Write your number of yes answers to questions 13 to 17: _____

There is a very good likelihood that you have PTSD if you indicated you have

1. at least one reexperiencing symptom (questions 1-5);

2. at least three numbing or avoidance symptoms (questions 6 to 12); and

3. at least two hyperarousal symptoms (questions 13 to 17).

If your numbers do not quite add up to at least 1, 3, and 2, you may still be experiencing post-traumatic stress to some degree. At the same time, only a trained mental health professional can formally diagnose you or anyone else as having PTSD.

If you are having PTSD symptoms, we are not surprised. When women have been abused, they often have these problems. You may wonder, "How do you know so much about me? Have you been talking to someone who knows me?" After all, we could just as easily have written that we bet you get upset when you are reminded of the abuse. We bet you don't like thinking about what happened. We bet you have trouble concentrating or sleeping. We bet you feel guilty about something that happened related to the abuse.

Of course, we know nothing about you and know very little about our therapy clients when we first meet them in our office. We do not know anything about their intelligence, their spirituality, their character, their determination, or their motivation to overcome or solve their problems. But we do know something about them because we know they have experienced some really bad things. And we know something about you. We know that you have been physically or psychologically abused by an intimate partner, and you have probably also experienced other bad things—such as a serious accident, the sudden and unexpected death of a loved one, or physical or sexual abuse while growing up.

From this point on, we will be writing as if you, the reader, are in fact suffering from PTSD. In so doing, we will be addressing you in much the same ways as we talk to our battered women clients in cognitive trauma therapy.

Some Important Facts about PTSD

If you are experiencing some or many of the symptoms of PTSD, it is not a reflection on your personality or on your ability to cope with or recover from adversity. You are having these problems because of what happened to you. PTSD symptoms are normal human reactions to extreme or pathological stress. These problems are common for people who have experienced highly traumatic events.

In one study, a group of rape victims were assessed in the emergency room right after the rape and then assessed again every week for three months. Two weeks after the rape, 94 percent of these women met symptomatic criteria for PTSD, and three months after the rape, 47 percent had PTSD (Rothbaum et al. 1992). In a nationwide study of Vietnam veterans, almost two in five who had considerable exposure to combat (35.8 percent) met full diagnostic criteria for PTSD fifteen to twenty years after their tours in Vietnam (Kulka et al. 1990).

These two studies also illustrate that when PTSD is severe it does not ordinarily go away with the mere passage of time. The adage "time heals" does not apply to PTSD when it is severe. For example, in the study of rape victims (described above), if symptoms had not started to subside by the fourth week after the rape, they had still not subsided after three months. Telling a formerly battered woman to "put it behind you and get on with your life" will usually do far more harm than good because most people do not know how to get over severe PTSD. If she could get on with her life, she would! Similarly, the worst thing you can say to yourself is something like, "Why can't I get over this? There must be something wrong with me."

In a study of 255 women with histories of physical and/or sexual abuse (most of whom had sought counseling for the abuse), 80 percent had PTSD. Similarly, in a study of women in support groups for battered women, 80 percent had PTSD (Kubany et al. 2000). Imagine yourself in a support group with ten other battered women. If this group was representative—eight of the ten other women in your group would have PTSD! If you have PTSD, you are definitely not alone. In fact, if someone else had the same trauma history as you, they would probably have PTSD too.

Many batterers tell their wives or girlfriends that they are "crazy." And many of our battered women clients have told us early in therapy, "I *feel* like I'm going crazy." It is important for you to know that trauma does not cause or produce serious mental illness. If you have PTSD, it does not mean that you are either crazy or going crazy.

PTSD is learned. It is not a disease or an illness like the flu. PTSD is acquired according to psychological learning principles, including Pavlovian or emotional conditioning and operant or reward conditioning. In other words, PTSD can be understood in terms of learned maladaptive emotions and avoidance. And because PTSD is learned, it can be unlearned according to the same principles that account for its acquisition and persistence. Therefore, we do not refer to the battered women that we see in therapy as *patients*. They are not sick. Instead, we refer to the people that we see in therapy as *clients*. And we tell clients that we could just as easily refer to them as *students* and ourselves as *teachers* because our therapy relies primarily on teaching and education. At the end of our therapy program, when we ask clients to give an overall evaluation of their therapy experience, they often say things such as "I learned so much from these classes."

Finally, even though PTSD is listed in *DSM-IV* as an anxiety disorder, PTSD is not a mood disorder. PTSD can be best understood as a cognitive or thinking problem. How you think affects how you feel, and if you change how you think, you will feel better. In PTSD, the meaning the trauma has for you has everything to do with the extent to which you will recover from the effects of traumatization. There's some good news and some bad news here. The bad news is that we can't change what happened to you. We wish that we could, but we cannot. The good news is that we may be able to help you change your interpretation of what happened, which is another way of making you feel much better.

PTSD Symptoms

Now, we are going to elaborate upon the different types of PTSD symptoms. This workbook will give you techniques for addressing all of these problems.

Reexperiencing Symptoms

There are five reexperiencing symptoms:

- unwanted thoughts or images of the abuse even though nothing is happening to remind you

- distress or emotional upset when something happens that is a reminder of the abuse

- distressing dreams or nightmares about the abuse

- suddenly reliving the abuse, flashbacks of the abuse, or acting or feeling as if the abuse is happening again

- having physical reactions when reminded of the abuse (such as sweating, breathing rapidly, a pounding heart, a queasy stomach, muscle tension)

All of the reexperiencing symptoms involve distressing recollections of the trauma. Many different abuse reminders are distressing for formerly battered women—such as violence on TV or in the movies and articles about violence in newspapers and magazines. It is also often distressing for formerly battered women to talk about, think about, or hear about the abuse. If you have had a reexperiencing symptom related to partner abuse in the past month, describe an example of the situation and what happened:

_____

_____

Avoidance Symptoms

There are three avoidance symptoms:

- efforts to avoid thoughts, feelings, or conversations that remind you of the abuse

- efforts to avoid activities, people, or places that remind you of the abuse

- inability to recall some important part(s) of the abuse

On the one hand, you may be unable to keep recollections of the trauma out of your mind. On the other hand, you may have been constantly trying to keep memories or recollections of the trauma out of your mind—pushing them down, putting them away, stuffing. You probably don't want to go there.

The first two avoidance symptoms involve very conscious or deliberate avoidance. You don't like thinking about the abuse and avoid doing things or engaging in activities that will remind you. What is something you have been avoiding, and what kinds of efforts do you make to avoid it?

_____

_____

The third avoidance symptom is involuntary avoidance: amnesia for some important aspect of the abuse or other trauma. This kind of avoidance does not involve normal forgetting. It is more like a memory block of something you would ordinarily remember. For example, you might be unable to remember a really bad or even horrific experience.

Many survivors of serious childhood physical or sexual abuse have amnesia for childhood trauma—but the amnesia may have enabled them to function—a form of emotion-focused coping. About twenty-five years ago in a U.S. city, children with documented incidents of childhood sexual abuse were examined at the emergency room. Twenty years later, 120 women were interviewed for a study but were not told the true purpose of the study. Thirty-eight percent of these women could not recall the incident that had brought them to the emergency room as children (Williams 1994).

Numbing Symptoms

There are four numbing symptoms:

- loss of interest in activities that were important to you—such as your job, school, hobbies, sports, or social activities

- feeling detached or cut off from other people

- feeling emotionally numb (for example, an inability to feel tenderness, loving feelings, or joyful feelings, or an inability to cry)

- thinking your future will be cut short in some way—such as no expectation of a career, marriage, or children; thinking that you will die prematurely

The numbing symptoms are very depression-like—loss of interest in activities that used to be enjoyable, feeling detached or cut off from others. Numbing may be experienced as an emotional deadness that inhibits positive feelings, happy feelings, joyful feelings, spontaneous laughter, or the ability to cry. If you have had any of the numbing symptoms in the past month, describe an example of the situation and what happened:

_____

_____

PTSD and depression tend to go together. That is, people who have PTSD tend to be depressed, and the more severe the PTSD, the more severe the depression tends to be. For example, if you see someone who has experienced some trauma and they look depressed, it is highly likely they are also suffering from PTSD. In a study with fifty women who were living in a shelter for battered women, seven of these women were severely depressed and all seven of these women had PTSD (Kubany et al. 1995a). The good news here is that, in our experience, the depression is secondary to the PTSD. If you get rid of your PTSD, your depression will lift.

In our view, the numbness represents a way of protecting you from experiencing the pain associated with some loss—with an associated inability to accept and grieve some loss.

Hyperarousal Symptoms

There are five hyperarousal symptoms:

- trouble falling or staying asleep

- feeling irritable or angry

- difficulty concentrating

- being hyperalert, watchful, or on guard (looking around yourself, checking out noises, checking windows and doors to be sure they are locked)

- feeling jumpy or easily startled by sounds or sudden movements

People with PTSD are overaroused or hyperaroused. It is as if, when you get up in the morning, you feel like you have already had three cups of coffee. There is even some evidence that individuals with PTSD may have higher resting heart rates than individuals without PTSD (Muraoka, Carlson, and Chemtob 1998). As a result of the hyperarousal, they are probably overreactive. They have difficulty concentrating because they are too aroused. You may overreact to sudden sounds because you are overaroused. You may have trouble relaxing and sleeping because you are overaroused. If you have had any of the reexperiencing symptoms, describe an example of the situation and what happened:

Anger is one hyperarousal symptom that many women with PTSD manifest or express differently from men—especially Vietnam combat veterans—many of whom are very angry and verbally aggressive. Many women with PTSD don't like arguments or raised voices, and they avoid conflict at all costs. Anger and conflict are avoided for two reasons. First, arguments and raised voices are reminders of the trauma and getting hurt. By avoiding conflict, you are engaging in a PTSD avoidance symptom—avoidance of activities that serve as reminders of the trauma.

What do arguments and raised voices remind you of?

Second, you may also be avoiding anger and conflict to avoid negative consequences. In the past, you may have been verbally abused or hit when you expressed anger or dissatisfaction. As a result, an impulse to express dissatisfaction may now make you anxious or fearful, so you consciously suppress impulses to speak up, disagree, argue, or express anger.

When you got fed up and expressed dissatisfaction to your abusive partner, what happened?

Trauma-Related Guilt, Anger, and Grief

You may have noticed that questions 18 to 20 in the PTSD Questionnaire didn't correspond to the above series of symptoms; that's because trauma-related guilt, trauma-related anger, and trauma-related grief are not currently considered core symptoms of PTSD in *DSM-IV*. But they should be—because when these three problems are resolved, PTSD usually goes away. In other words, when trauma-related guilt, anger, and grief are no longer problematic issues for a trauma survivor, the individual rarely has PTSD anymore.

If you have guilt that relates to the abuse in some way, what is something you feel guilty about?

_____

_____

Guilt is a big problem for almost all battered women with PTSD, and we devote chapters 9 and 10 to teaching you about guilt and to helping you get rid of your guilt.

If you have anger that relates to the abuse in some way, what is something you feel angry about?

_____

_____

In guilt, the finger is pointed at yourself. In anger, the finger is pointed at someone else—for example, the batterer or the judicial system. Anger is not as big a problem for battered women as is guilt, but we devote chapter 3 to helping you let go of any anger you may have.

What losses were associated with your abuse?

_____

_____

In trauma, there are two kinds of losses—tangible losses and symbolic losses. Tangible losses can include losses of property or possessions, permanent injuries, scars, or losses of custody of the children. Symbolic losses can be just as significant—such as loss of identity, loss of self-worth, loss of faith in human nature, loss of optimism, loss of time, loss of innocence, loss of control, loss of trust, or loss of a marital dream of growing old with your "soul mate" as an intact family.

How PTSD Develops and How It Affects You

In this section, we are going to explain how factors that have nothing to do with you contribute to PTSD, how PTSD develops, why people with PTSD have many shared experiences, and why memories of long-past trauma may still cause you pain. Understanding this process may help you make sense out of what you have been going through.

External Factors

Certain situational factors make some negative events more stressful than others and make some traumatic events more traumatic than others. That is, any factor or situation that causes a person to experience intense distress will increase chances that the person will develop PTSD.

Only stressful events that evoke intensely negative reactions—such as terror, horror, or perceptions of complete helplessness—are likely to cause PTSD. Events that evoke less intense emotional reactions are unlikely to produce PTSD. For example, stressful events such as a divorce, loss of a job, or chronic illness leading to death of an elderly parent do not ordinarily result in PTSD. Understanding the role that these situational factors play in the development of PTSD may help you understand why PTSD has far more to do with the type of stressor to which you have been exposed than with anything about you or your personality.

Degree of Damage or Harm

First, the most important determinant of how much distress a negative event will cause is the amount of damage or harm caused by the event. The greater the damage or harm a stressful event causes, the greater will be the distress. For example, if someone dies in an accident, distress among the survivors will be more severe than if someone is only injured. According to the *DSM-IV*, the types of stressors that can result in PTSD include "experiencing or witnessing an event or events involving actual or threatened death or serious injury to self or others" (American Psychiatric Association 1994, p. 427). Such events are likely to evoke intense distress in almost anyone. Many batterers threaten to kill their girlfriends or wives, and this can be extraordinarily traumatic, whether or not the women are ever hit by their partners.

Similarly, severely damaging events which occur over and over can contribute cumulatively to the amount of distress experienced by individuals who have been exposed to these events. Among battered women who have been abused over and over again over long periods of time, fear is often not only intense but also chronic, and it is no surprise that many such women suffer from severe PTSD. Similarly, it is no surprise that many combat veterans who were exposed to repeated life-threatening stressors while in the war zone developed PTSD.

Proximity to Harm

A second external factor which contributes to how much distress a stressful event will cause is a person's proximity, or closeness, to the stressful event. One kind of proximity is geographical closeness. Almost anyone would be more upset if they witnessed a really bad accident than if they just heard about it. A second kind of proximity is emotional closeness to someone who has experienced a negative event. If something really bad happens to someone with whom you are emotionally close—such as a family member or other loved one—distress is likely to be extreme. For example, many battered women experience intense distress if their children witness the violence or if the children are direct victims of the violence themselves.

Negative Events That Happen Out of the Blue

A third external factor that contributes to how much distress a negative event will cause is the degree to which the stressor is completely unexpected and shatters basic assumptions about safety and predictability. Battery can be a shockingly negative event that occurs without any warning and does not make any sense or fit your view of how the world is supposed to work. Consider an example of a woman whose previously loving boyfriend hit her and broke her jaw out of the blue. Her response was, "I can't believe this happened . . . Something like this isn't supposed to happen . . . This should never have happened . . . It doesn't make any sense . . . Why would he do this to me?"

People-Caused Negative Events vs. Acts of God

A fourth external factor that contributes to how much distress a negative event will cause is whether the damage is caused by other people or caused by something perceived to be outside of human control (due to chance or bad luck or acts of God, such as natural disasters). Human-caused negative events produce more distress than negative events outside human control because human-caused negative events are much more likely to generate guilt and anger—which exacerbate or worsen the impact of the events. That is, individuals who are impacted by a natural disaster, such as a hurricane, are much less likely to point fingers of blame (at themselves or someone else) than are victims of violent crime. Trauma-related guilt and anger can be huge sources of torment or emotional pain, which can be extremely long lasting and endure long after the traumatic event or events are over.

Consider the following scenario. A woman was beaten severely on multiple occasions by her husband of several years—the man with whom she fell in love as her "prince charming" and with whom she thought she would grow old, as her "soul mate." Here was her response: "How could someone who is supposed to love me and protect me betray me and be so mean and cruel? How could this have happened? It doesn't make any sense. Why did I marry him? I never should have married him. I should have left him the first time he hit me. How could anyone be so cruel! Why on earth did he do that? He never should have treated me that way!"

Can you see how much emotional pain the trauma of senseless domestic violence has caused and why this woman may be suffering from PTSD? The stories of many of the women with whom we have worked are similar to this one.

Trying to Figure Out Why It Happened

When trauma is occurring, victims are frequently in a state of shock or disbelief. They find it hard to believe what is happening and are often terrified and horrified. It's like your heart is racing at ninety miles an hour, like pressing the accelerator to the floor when the car is in idle. Now, it's after the trauma, and you're safe. But you are still agitated, still very upset. It's like taking your foot off the gas pedal, but the pedal doesn't come all the way back up.

When really bad things happen, people try to make sense out of what happened, to understand why it happened. If you know why something happened, maybe you can predict when it is likely to happen again and can prevent it from happening again. It is human nature and even animal nature to search for meaning in negative events. If we drop a mouse on the floor, the first thing the mouse will do is explore the room—to anchor herself in space, to make the environment predictable. People and animals don't like uncertainty or ambiguity. It is a universal tendency for animals and humans to act in ways that reduce uncertainty and increase predictability.

What kinds of questions do people ask when they try to make sense out of unthinkably bad events and try to understand why the events happened? Or, more specifically, what kinds of questions have you asked yourself to try to make sense of your partner's verbal abuse and/or violence?

_____

_____

In all likelihood you wanted to know what led to the abuse, and you may blame yourself. For many women, the question "Why did I do what I did?" is followed by the statement, "I shouldn't have done what I did," and this reflects guilt because the thought "I shouldn't have . . . " is usually associated with emotional pain. Guilt is an unpleasant feeling with accompanying beliefs that one should have thought, felt, or acted differently (Kubany and Watson 2003). The question "Why did he do what he did?" is often followed by the statement "He shouldn't have done that"—and this reflects anger because the thought "He shouldn't have . . . " is usually associated with emotional pain. Anger is an unpleasant feeling with accompanying beliefs that someone else should have thought, felt, or acted differently. In guilt, the finger of responsibility is pointed at one's self. In anger, the finger of responsibility is pointed at someone else.

Why Guilt?

It is because trauma survivors are constantly asking "why" that guilt and anger are extremely common among trauma survivors. Trauma is a fertile breeding ground for both guilt and anger. In fact, guilt is a symptom of PTSD just like fever is a symptom of an infection. In a study of 168 individuals in support groups for battered women, only 6 of these women experienced no guilt related to their victimization (Kubany et al. 1996). Trauma survivors will experience guilt whether they deserve to or not, and usually they do not.

Guilt is usually more important than anger in PTSD because we believe guilt contributes directly to shame, low self-esteem, depression, and social isolation. If you feel guilty and ashamed, how high can your self-esteem be? Not very high. If your self-esteem is low, you will also feel depressed. And if you feel ashamed and depressed, you probably will want to be alone and want to withdraw or isolate yourself.

Why Anger?

"How could he? . . . He shouldn't have . . . How could someone who is supposed to nurture and protect me hurt me? . . . Why would he do that? . . . That SOB!" Multiple victimizations or multiple betrayals can lead to mistrust, cynicism, and hostile world views—negative views about human nature and religion. If you can't trust your husband, or your boyfriend, or your stepfather, how can you trust any man? Not trusting other people leads to social isolation.

Why You?

"Why did this happen to me? . . . Why would God do this to me? . . . What did I do to deserve this? . . . What goes around comes around? . . . Am I hexed? . . . Am I jinxed?" Have you asked yourself questions like these? The only answer really is bad luck: wrong place, wrong time. What happened to you was tragic, and you didn't deserve it. You were just unlucky.

There was a woman who went through the San Francisco earthquake and was terribly traumatized. She moved to Los Angeles and was right in the middle of the Los Angeles riots. In September 1992, she went to the island of Kauai in Hawaii for a vacation. Do you know what happened on Kauai on September 11, 1992? Hurricane Iniki. This woman said she was a "basket case" when they escorted her off the island. She thought erroneously—because of this incredible coincidence—that these disasters had something to do with her. But this was just really really bad luck.

Military combatants who are the least traumatized by warfare and least likely to have PTSD know that what happened was just bad luck: "War is hell . . . In war, people die . . . Why did my buddy die? He was unlucky. He didn't deserve to die, it didn't make any sense, and it was tragic. But, it didn't have anything to do with me."

Emotional Numbing and the Persistence of PTSD

"Why" questions that search for meaning in senseless events—where there are no good answers—often lead to emotional numbing. This numbing is a protective barrier that keeps you from experiencing the pain of loss—preventing the grieving and acceptance of the loss.

Guilt and anger can contribute to the persistence of the numbing. Guilt can be so painful, many survivors do not like to think about what happened. But if you don't think about what happened, how can you reprocess what happened and grieve the loss? You can't.

Anger is the only emotion you can experience that is compatible with numbing. Have you been to a funeral lately? Do people scream or cry at funerals? They cry. Unlike anger, weeping and sobbing are not self-defense reactions. In fact, there is some evidence that anger may interfere with the grieving process. In a study of trauma reexperiencing therapy, anger interfered with recovery (Foa, Riggs, and Massie 1995).

Psychological Shocks That Perpetuate Pain from the Past

Sometimes clients ask, "Why can't I get over it? It happened so long ago!" It's something like this: Have you ever been to a karaoke bar? (In karaoke bars, people sing songs with the words of the song on a TV screen so you can sing along—even if you don't know the song.) Let's say you go to the bar to sing and to distract yourself from your trauma. As you turn on the TV, notice that they are not playing any songs. They are playing your trauma. And the ticker tape of words on top are saying: "I could have prevented this. I never should gone out with him. I should have left sooner. How stupid! That monster. How could he be so cruel? How could anyone who is supposed to love me do that to me?"

These emotionally charged words, which make you feel bad, are psychological shocks that recharge the images with negative energy. This is why memories of the trauma may never lose their ability to make us feel bad—even after many years.

How Does This Model of PTSD Fit for You?

Describe how well this portrait of PTSD describes what you have been going through. If it doesn't fit you perfectly, what doesn't fit?

_____

_____

_____

_____

What Did You Learn Today?

At the end of every session in cognitive trauma therapy, we ask clients, "What did you learn today?" or "What did you get out of today's session?" We do this to bring to the forefront of our clients' minds the highlights of the session or the most important learning that occurred in the session. We are going to employ a similar format in this workbook.

What is something you learned from reading this chapter, answering the questions, and doing the exercises?

_____

_____

_____

CHAPTER 2

Self-Advocacy: An Overview and Initial Self-Assessment

To advocate for someone is to act on someone's behalf. Advocates act on their clients' behalf by acting in their best interest and by promoting their long-term happiness. Think of yourself as if you were your own client. Are you a good advocate for yourself? Would you hire someone to advocate for you the way you have been advocating for yourself?

When Self-Advocacy Is Lacking

In our therapy with battered women, some similar problem areas come up over and over again with different clients. These problem areas are in five styles of functioning that are all interrelated and reflect a lack of self-advocacy, and a lack of self-advocacy contributes to low self-esteem, depression, and your needs not getting met. These styles of functioning are briefly described and discussed below.

Placing Other People's Wants Ahead of Your Own

In our experience, many women with PTSD repeatedly place the needs and wants of other people ahead of their own. Most of these women (and perhaps you too) have spent a large part of their lives taking care of other people, trying to put out fires, and trying to anticipate and avoid disapproval. When they put themselves first, they feel selfish, rude, and guilty. This has to change, because if you don't put yourself first, who will? It is very important that you become your own strongest advocate.

Unassertiveness and Tolerance of Disrespect

A second problem area, closely related to the first, is being unassertive. Women with PTSD are unwilling or unable to communicate their wants directly to others, and they may be willing to tolerate an inordinate amount of disrespectful treatment from others.

Decision Making Driven by "Supposed Tos"

A third common problem area is that decision-making processes are dictated or driven by a multiplicity of "supposed to," "should," or "have to" beliefs of obligation. These "supposed to" beliefs foster decisions that are more likely to serve the wants or interests of other people, often at your expense. Women with PTSD are unlikely to make important decisions based on a rational analysis of what course of action is most likely to be in their best interest or most likely to promote their long-term happiness. For example, many battered women have stayed in or returned to an abusive relationship because they thought they should, had to, or were supposed to—out of a sense of obligation. Had they made these decisions based on a rational analysis of what course of action was most likely to be in their and their children's best interest, many of these women would have left their abusers sooner and would have been less likely to reconcile after they had left.

Inability to Deal with Hostility

A fourth interrelated problem area that is all too common is a tendency for battered women to be threatened and intimidated by aggressive people, and their feelings are often deeply hurt by nasty and hurtful comments spoken by family, friends, former partners, and others. They are unable to defend themselves against the hostile and hurtful verbal assaults of other people. For example, one woman, whose husband called her "spiritually hollow," said nothing but was devastated by what he had said, and her self-esteem was shattered. As another example, when one woman was asked by her husband, "Why are you so selfish and needy?" she answered, "I don't know." It never occurred to her to say something like, "That's not a nice thing to say, and I don't deserve to be talked to that way."

Negative Self-Talk

A fifth interrelated problem area shared by many women who have been battered is that they are often their own worst enemy. They mistreat themselves by saying and thinking things that are just as disrespectful as their abusive partners were. Consider the following statements, which are similar to what we often hear early in our therapy with battered women. "I should have known better . . . I could have prevented it . . . I have bad judgement . . . There's something wrong with me . . . I'm stupid . . . I'm a loser . . . I'm a fool." Negative self-talk—in thoughts and speech—contributes to depression, to low self-esteem, and to a sense of shame.

Because these issues come up over and over again in our therapy with battered women, we found ourselves saying the same things over and over again to our clients, asking them to examine how their beliefs and ways of relating to themselves and other people contribute to their own unhappiness, depression, and low self-esteem. Eventually we developed a standard repertoire of brief responses.

Here is one example:

Client: I should have known better. I wasted five years of my life. I could have prevented all that suffering.

Therapist: If you never say "could have" or "should have" again, you will be a happier person.

Clients who came to believe these statements and started acting on them became more efficacious, took charge of their lives, and gained greater personal control of their future happiness. These statements became self-advocacy strategies, or guidelines for getting their wants and needs met. A strategy is an overall plan of action for accomplishing some long-term objective. Self-advocacy strategies are ways of thinking and acting that promote your best interest. Now we are going to give you the opportunity to assess your beliefs with respect to twenty-five self-advocacy strategies by completing the following Self-Advocacy Strategies Questionnaire.

Self-Advocacy Strategies Questionnaire

Instructions: To recover fully from the effects of trauma, you need to become your own strongest advocate. Listed below are twenty-five self-advocacy strategies that will help you to promote your best interests and empower yourself. If you adopt or embrace and come to live by these statements, your recovery from trauma will go forward at a rapid pace.

First, read through the entire questionnaire. Then, read each statement again and write down what this statement means to you. Is it true for you? If not, do you want it to be true? How does or could this self-advocacy strategy help you?

Today's Date: _____

1. "Getting my wants and needs satisfied is more important than satisfying the needs of someone else. I need to make my best interests and wants a top priority. (Advocating for my best interest means to do things and make decisions that promote the long-term happiness and quality of life for me and my children.)" What do you believe about these statements and how they are relevant for you?

   _____

   _____

2. "Getting my wants and needs satisfied belongs at the top of my daily to do list. If I don't put myself first, who will? If I get my needs satisfied, I will have more energy to satisfy the wants and needs of others." What do you believe about these statements and how they are relevant for you?

   _____

   _____

3. "It does not promote my long-term happiness to think or talk about things that I cannot change—such as dwelling on the unfairness of the system or past injustices. The time I spend on such things is time I cannot spend working on things I can control, change, or do something about. Time spent doing things of little value costs me the opportunity of spending that time doing something that is more worthwhile. In other words, spending time on things I can't change does not belong on my daily 'to do' list!"

   _____

   _____

4. "To get my needs met, I need to tell people how I feel and what I want. Other people cannot read my mind and won't know how I feel or what I want unless I tell them."

   _____

   _____

5. "I need to stand up for my rights and not allow myself to be taken advantage of. I not only deserve respect, I must demand respect. (To demand respect means to not tolerate disrespect.)"

   _____

   _____

6. "I need to make decisions based on what is in my best interest (and my children's best interest). I need to stop doing things because I think I should. (The question to ask myself when trying to decide what to do is 'What course of action is most likely to promote my long-term happiness or quality of life?')"

---

7. "When I do something or make a decision in order to get immediate relief from painful feelings, chances are good that I am not acting in my best interest."

---

8. "If a decision will lead to either guilt or resentment, go with guilt! Because it is more likely I will be acting in my best interest rather than someone else's."

---

9. "Strong feelings associated with thoughts or ideas are not evidence that these ideas are correct (or incorrect). It is not in my best interest to make important decisions based on how I feel about things; important decisions should be made on the basis of the evidence and an intellectual analysis of what is in my best interest."

---

10. "Am I in a high state of distress (anxiety, worry, dread, depression) about an important decision I 'should' or 'have to' make? Any course of action that will give me immediate relief from this distress is not likely to be in my best interest. I need to achieve a state of calm before making any important decision. Otherwise, I may make an impulsive decision that is bad for me in the long run. I will be more objective and think more clearly if I am calm when I select my course of action."

---

11. "Just because somebody says that I have negative qualities does not mean it's true. However, I do not have control over the words that come out of other people's mouths. I just need to remember that words are just sound waves (not fists or baseball bats)."

---

12. "Just because someone blames me (or blamed me) does not mean it was my fault."

---

13. "Just because someone apologizes to me for some wrongdoing does not mean I am now obligated to do what that person wants or go back to the way things were (whether or not I forgive the person)."

_____

_____

14. "If I never say 'could have' or 'should have' again, I will be a happier person."

_____

_____

15. "Tearing myself down ('I'm worthless . . . I'm stupid . . . I'm never going to be happy,' etc.) makes me depressed and want to give up or go away. I need to start treating myself with the same respect that I would like to get—and deserve—from others."

_____

_____

16. "When talking about things I don't like about myself, it's much better to say 'this is the way I have been (or have done things) in the past' rather than 'this is the way I am or what I always do.' The latter implies that this is the way I am always going to be; the former implies that I can do things differently in the future."

_____

_____

17. "Just because I think a thought or have an idea does not mean the thought or idea is true. I need to stop automatically believing everything that comes into my mind. The thoughts may just be bad habits. I need to evaluate the evidence for some of the irrational ideas that pop into my mind."

_____

_____

18. "I need to stop saying 'I feel' this or that way with words that are not emotions (for example, 'I feel stuck, obligated, overwhelmed'). Instead, I need to examine the evidence for thinking that I am stuck, obligated, or overwhelmed. If I evaluate the evidence for these negative ideas, I may realize I'm not really stuck, obligated, overwhelmed, and so on."

_____

_____

19. "I need to stop asking 'why?' Knowing why will not change what happened, and it keeps me stuck in the past."

_____

_____

20. "I may have been helpless and out of control when I was abused by my partner or when I was a child; but I am not powerless or out of control now."

_____

_____

21. "If I focus on possible solutions to my problems, I may solve them. If I focus on reasons why my problems can't be solved, my problems will be solved only if I get lucky."

_____

_____

22. "I am an innocent survivor and am likable and lovable. I also deserve to be happy."

_____

_____

23. "When a woman says, 'I feel sorry for him,' she is making the other person's problem her problem. If I feel sorry for him, I'm supposed to do something about it. I should do something that he would like me to do (go back to him; stay in the relationship). This is faulty thinking! I may not like to see him suffer, but it may be contrary to my best interest to do something that reduces my guilt and alleviates his 'pain.' I am not responsible for solving the problems that he caused and for which he needs to be held accountable. (Otherwise, he'll never learn and will continue to treat other women the way he treated me.) If I do something that he wants because I feel sorry for him, it means that I may be placing his wants and interests above my own (and my children's) best interest. I must act in my best interest."

_____

_____

24. "When someone says, 'I had to,' it usually means she chose to. Ordinarily, only children, slaves, prisoners, and people threatened with violence have to comply. In most cases, when we do something that somebody expects us to do, even when we don't want to do it, we choose to do it. I am not going to get physically hurt if I do not comply with a request or demand! I can choose to say no. This distinction is important because when I have choices, I have power and am in control. When I perceive myself as not having choices ('I had to'), I am powerless and out of control. For example, when I say someone is 'taking advantage of me,' it usually means that I am allowing that person to take advantage. This latter phrase implies that I can do something to stop unfair treatment and prevent it from happening in the future."

_____

_____

25. "When I get out of bed tomorrow, who is going to decide whether or not I am going to have a good day? Me or someone else? Of course, I want to be the one who decides. However, if I'm hoping that someone doesn't ruin my day by treating me in a certain way, I am going to have a good day only if I get lucky, like being in a rudderless boat praying that a friendly wind will blow me ashore rather than out to

sea. On the other hand, if I know I am going to have a good day, no matter what (or in spite of what) someone else says or does, I am in control of my well-being."

Self-Advocacy: How You May Change

In our therapy with battered women, we used to assign the above exercise only once—before the last session, when we conduct a session on self-advocacy. Now we assign the self-advocacy exercise for homework at the first session, which gives many clients a road map of what they want to accomplish in therapy. Then, we ask them to complete the exercise once again before the last session. When they first complete the questionnaire, most clients acknowledge that they haven't been living their lives according to these strategies and admit to not knowing how to implement them. At the same time, they see that these strategies make sense.

In the chapters that follow, we will give you information that will strengthen your beliefs about the importance of self-advocacy and help you put self-advocacy strategies into practice. When you get to the last chapter, we will ask you to fill out this questionnaire again. If you are like most of the women who have completed cognitive trauma therapy, your ability to implement self-advocacy strategies will have increased significantly, and your self-confidence will also have increased. If you come to embrace our self-advocacy strategies as important guidelines for conducting your life affairs, we believe that your self-esteem will increase, and you will be a happier person.

To give you an idea of what may be possible for you in the way of self-advocacy, we are now going to repeat the first two self-advocacy statements, along with one woman's responses, completed after the first session of cognitive trauma therapy and then completed again before the last therapy session.

1. "Getting my wants and needs satisfied is more important than satisfying the needs of someone else. I need to make my best interests and wants a top priority."

After first session: "This is very important to me because I have always put the needs of my children and others above mine, but I have oftentimes been unhappy in the end when I try to do things for myself, I feel selfish and guilty."

Before last session: "This is of utmost importance. If I don't advocate for myself, who will? I like this feeling immensely! It makes me feel happier. I've changed!"

2. "Getting my wants and needs satisfied belongs at the top of my daily to do list. If I don't make myself first, who will? If I get my needs satisfied, I will have more energy to satisfy the wants and needs of others."

After first session: "Extremely important to make myself first. I haven't done this in my entire life. This is new to me."

Before last session: "When I make myself first on my list of to dos, I am happier and am able to satisfy and give more to others. I like being number one and I don't feel guilty either. I feel good."

What do you think about the way this woman's answers changed between her first therapy session and her last therapy session?

_____

_____

She seems like a different person, doesn't she? Would you like to change like this woman has changed and become the type of woman she is today? We think you can! And reading (and perhaps rereading) these strategies may give you a road map of where you want to go with your life and the type of person you would like to become.

The self-advocacy strategies are available on laminated, magnetized cards, suitable for posting as visible self-advocacy reminders. The cards may be ordered on our Web site: www.healingthetrauma.com.

What did you learn from reading this chapter and completing the self-advocacy exercise?

_____

_____

_____

_____

CHAPTER 3

Is Anger Worth the Hangover?
Strategies for Letting Go

If you are angry at your abuser for what he did, or are angry at the police or judicial system for letting you down, or are mad at someone else who did something they shouldn't have done, your anger is interfering with your recovery from PTSD—whether or not you have a right to be angry.

Is Anger Ever Healthy or Beneficial?

The point is not whether your anger is legitimate or justified—in the sense that the target of your anger may very well deserve some kind of punishment. To stop being angry is not letting someone off the hook. They may still deserve punishment. But if you are holding onto your anger or are reluctant to let go, it is unlikely that you are sufficiently motivated to learn how to break the anger habit and to stop being angry.

Some therapists and victim services providers believe that anger is a healthy and adaptive emotion for battered women who are safely out of an abusive relationship. Chronic abuse can leave some women so completely numb that they are unable to express any kind of negative feelings and continue to tolerate violations of their rights.

Feeling, if not expressing, anger is a healthy response when it stirs a woman to get out of an abusive relationship. We also believe that it is far better to express anger than to keep all negative feelings bottled up inside. Keeping negative feelings bottled up almost always contributes to depression and feelings of low self-worth. In this way, anger may be seen as a healthy, transitory bridge to reempowerment and, to some extent, as a relief from depression. To recover from your PTSD, it is essential that you be able to experience unpleasant feelings and be able to express dissatisfaction. If you can't get in touch with negative feelings, you may be unwittingly allowing yourself to tolerate being treated with disrespect. However, it is very important for you to know that you do not have to express anger to express dissatisfaction or negative feelings. Please read on.

Most anger is a secondary emotional experience. It is secondary in that it is usually a reaction to a more fundamental emotional experience. Anger is usually a strategy for dealing with this more fundamental experience. For example, anger is often a reaction to some kind of frustration or thwarted need.

In chapter 12, which is on assertiveness, we will emphasize the importance of expressing dissatisfaction in terms of distress ("I'm upset . . . I'm frustrated . . . My feelings are hurt"), which is more likely to direct the focus of your thoughts and conversation on the problem (and how it can be solved) rather than on the person who is the source of the problem. We will also discuss the importance of expressing your wants and needs in a very direct, assertive, but nonaggressive manner. A major problem associated with the expression of anger is that expressing anger typically escalates conflict and alienates the person who is the target of the anger (Kubany et al. 1995b). Expressing anger is unlikely to influence the target of your anger in a positive way.

Chronic Anger and Health

One last thing about anger: If you let go of your anger, you will probably live longer because the chronic personality pattern of "cynical hostility" is a risk factor for a variety of medical problems and premature death (Friedman 1992, p. 38).

Strategies for Letting Go

In cognitive trauma therapy, we give clients a homework assignment that challenges the way they may think about anger and provides tips or strategies for letting go of anger and breaking the anger habit. The ideas conveyed in this exercise appeal to most clients and typically increase their motivation to gain control over their emotions and to let go of their anger. Even if you aren't angry, we think that this letting go of anger exercise will increase your awareness or understanding of why anger is often toxic for battered women who experience anger.

Letting Go Exercise

This exercise contains ten statements. After you read each statement, please answer the question posed.

1. If you get angry about what someone else did (or continues to do), that person is still controlling your feelings (that is, they are still able to make you feel bad).

   Do you want this person to be able to control how you feel?

   _____

2. Anger and resentment do more damage to the container in which they are stored than to the object on which they are poured.

   What do you believe about this statement and how is it relevant for you?

   _____

   _____

3. In some ways, getting angry (or resenting someone) is like taking poison and waiting for someone else to die.

   What do you believe about this statement and how is it relevant for you?

   _____

   _____

4. To *forgive* means to pardon. To *pardon* means to release from punishment. If you pardon a guilty person, it does not excuse the person for his crimes or suggest they did not occur. It only means that continued punishment is not worth the energy and cost that would be required.

   Would you want to spend the rest of your life as your ex-partner's jailer or warden? What kind of life would that be?

   _____

   _____

5. Would you put "spending time being angry" on your daily to do list? Will getting angry improve your day or improve your future? If it's only going to make you feel worse, you need to take it off of your to do list. If getting angry is not going to improve your day, getting angry is not in your best interest.

   What do you believe about these statements and how are they relevant for you?

   _____

   _____

6. Letting go of anger simply involves a decision. Anger requires rumination. Anger requires a memory or thought about unfair treatment, often accompanied by thoughts of wanting to hurt someone or see them suffer. In other words, anger is a choice or decision to continue ruminating. And because it's a choice, your anger is controllable. You can choose to stop being angry. If you make a decision to stop ruminating or obsessing about unfairness, you will start breaking the anger habit. Change the subject! It doesn't belong in your head.

   What do you believe about these statements and how are they relevant for you?

   _____

   _____

7. Immediately after asking why you (or a loved one) has been treated unfairly, you should ask yourself a second question—a *what* question: "What am I going to do about it?" If the answer is "I'm not going to do anything" (to improve the situation), you are wasting your time. You need to make a decision to change the subject and stop ruminating or obsessing in a way that just makes you feel bad. (There are no satisfying answers to the question "why?" What happened may have been tragic, and you didn't deserve it. You were just unlucky.)

   What do you believe about these statements and how are they relevant for you?

   _____

   _____

8. "There's no justice! . . . It's not fair . . . I was set up . . . deceived! . . . How dare he/they!? . . . How could anyone be so cruel? . . . Why would someone do something like that? . . . It never should have happened! . . . That pig . . . I hate his guts . . . I hope he rots in hell!" Feel better now? Probably not—or if so, just temporarily. Using emotionally charged words that convey anger and hostility only makes you feel bad and doesn't solve anything. When thinking about a perpetrator or some injustice, you will feel better if you use neutral or descriptive rather than emotionally charged or judgmental words.

   What do you believe about these statements and how are they relevant for you?

   _____

   _____

9. The next time you hear yourself saying or thinking, "I'm angry . . . mad . . . pissed off . . . resentful" you should change your wording to: "I'm frustrated" or "I'm upset" or "My feelings are hurt." What do angry people do? They fight, don't they? They say things that are hurtful, hostile, or downright mean. What do frustrated people

do? They focus on the obstacle or problem that is the source of the frustration. And that activates problem solving.

If you express anger toward someone who is the source of your frustration, will this increase the chances that the person will give you what you want or stop doing what you don't want them to do? No. Expressing anger usually escalates conflict and alienates the person who is the target of your anger.

What do you believe about these statements and how are they relevant for you?

_____

_____

10. Getting angry at someone who isn't even there with you is the ultimate act of futility. It's like having a prizefight with yourself; you will always end up losing.

    What do you believe about these statements and how are they relevant for you?

_____

_____

Before and After

In cognitive trauma therapy, we ask clients to complete the letting go of anger exercise at the beginning of therapy, as food for thought, and then again at the end of therapy. Here's an example of how one woman's responses changed over time. Listed below are her responses to the first two questions, first before and then after therapy.

1. If you get angry about what someone else did (or continues to do), that person is still controlling your feelings (that is, they are still able to make you feel bad). Do you want this person to be able to control how you feel?

Before first session: "No, but getting angry at him is the only way I can get the frustration out of my system."

Before last session: "No I don't because 'he who angers you, controls you.' It's not worth it."

2. Anger and resentment do more damage to the container in which they are stored than to the object on which they are poured.

Before first session: "This statement is true, but I think I'm the type of person to always hold resentment toward my ex-husband because he's done a lot to me, and he doesn't feel sorry for anything."

Before last session: "I believe this! Anger causes all kinds of side effects to the heart and blood pressure and mental health. The person I am aiming at feels no pain. Only I feel the pain."

Can you see how liberated this woman has become? By learning to let go of her anger, she is no longer controlled by her former abuser. She is more in control of her own future happiness. What about you? Are you going to be able to let go of your anger too?

_____

What did you learn from reading this chapter and completing the "letting go" of anger exercise?

_____

_____

_____

_____

CHAPTER 4

Feel Better by Changing the Way You Talk to Yourself

It is essential to your health and happiness that you start treating yourself with the same kind of respect that you would like to get—and deserve to get—from other people. The ways that you talk to yourself—the specific words you use when you think and speak—have a great deal to do with the speed with which you are going to recover from the effects of partner abuse as well as any other traumatic experiences you may have had.

The following are a sampling of the phrases from one of our clients who recorded them in a one-week period on a self-monitoring form. These phrases were all either thoughts that crossed her mind or words that came out of her mouth: "I'm going to lose it . . . I should have done it better . . . I am so stupid . . . I feel overwhelmed . . . Why did I ask him for help? I shouldn't have . . . I am so inadequate . . . I feel overwhelmed . . . I should have cleaned the house instead of going out . . . I am so irresponsible . . . I should have put the kids' lunch together last night . . . I'm a terrible mom . . . I feel like I can't make it . . . I feel like I'm going crazy."

Do her words sound familiar? Do you say things like this to yourself? ____

What do you know about this woman from her self-talk? She's not very happy, is she? She's depressed, isn't she? She's stressed out, isn't she? Her self-esteem isn't very high, is it? She doesn't think she is capable of solving her problems, does she? Is she treating herself with respect? Do you think she feels out of control? We would say so.

Does she deserve to be talked to this way, even by herself? ____

We certainly hope you said no. No one deserves to be talked to this way! How do you think those words made this woman feel? Not good, obviously. How do you think she would feel if someone else talked to her this way? In fact, how would *you* feel if someone talked to you this way? Let's see: "You're going to lose it . . . You should have done it better . . . You are so stupid . . . You're overwhelmed . . . Why did you ask him for help? You shouldn't have . . . You are so inadequate . . . You're overwhelmed . . . You should have cleaned the house instead of going out . . . You are so irresponsible . . . You should have put the kids' lunch together last night . . . You're a terrible mom . . . You can't make it . . . You're going crazy."

There's some good news and some bad news here. The bad news is that when you talk negatively to yourself, it has the same negative effect as when other people talk to you this way. The good news is that you have the potential or power to change the way that you talk to yourself. This is very important because recovery from PTSD requires that you treat yourself with the same respect that you would like to get from other people.

Treating yourself with respect is a form of self-advocacy. We want you to be your own strongest advocate and your own strongest cheering section by not tearing yourself down in any way.

Monitoring Your Negative Self-Talk

We have identified four categories of negative self-talk that are common for many battered women with PTSD. The first category includes statements using the word "should," the phrases "should have" and "could have," and "why" questions. Category 2 includes global, shame-related self-put-downs (slam dunks of your entire personality), like calling yourself "stupid" or "selfish." Category 3 is the most subtle and the most difficult to get a handle on. It includes all statements starting with "I feel" and ending with words that are not emotions, like "I feel obligated . . . I feel overwhelmed . . . I feel sorry for . . . I feel responsible." The feelings associated with the conclusions give the conclusions a false ring of truth. Saying "I feel" in sentences that end with words that are not emotions impairs or interferes with your ability to think clearly. For example, just because a woman "feels obligated" to forgive her abuser and give him another chance does not mean she is obligated to do so.

What is the fourth category of negative self-talk? Do you apologize very much? _____

Many of our clients say they apologize "all the time." One client said that she even says "I'm sorry" when she bumps into a chair. Apologizing all the time isn't good for you. You apologize to alleviate guilt or anxiety, correct? How would you feel if you didn't apologize? _____

What you get when you apologize is relief, and relief from anxiety or guilt is a very powerful reward. In states of pain, people will do almost anything to get relief. The truth is that these behaviors that lead to relief may be contributing to the persistence of your PTSD. We will discuss this topic again in chapter 7. For now let's look at some of the self-talk that you do.

Self-Monitoring Exercise

To break any habit, you need to increase your awareness of that habit. Awareness precedes change. One way to do this is by carefully observing and documenting the habit when it occurs. Research has shown that around-the-clock self-monitoring can aid in breaking a variety of habits, including negative ruminations (Korotitsch and Nelson-Gray 1999; Frederiksen 1975). To increase your awareness of your negative self-talk, we are going to teach you a method for keeping track of the four categories of negative self-talk that we described above.

The goal of this exercise during the first week is to increase your awareness of using these statements. The immediate goal is not to decrease their occurrence. Later, as you start becoming more aware, you will probably start to realize when you are about to say them. You will start catching yourself when you start to think or say these words, and this may interrupt a chain of negative self-talk, which in the past may have had a life of its own—of which you may not even have been aware. When you get to that stage, you might then be able to start using different words to express what you are trying to say.

You can use the self-monitoring forms at the end of this section. The goal is to estimate the amount of negative self-talk you engage in weekly for six consecutive weeks. If you diligently keep track of and document your negative self-talk, we can almost guarantee that you will be treating yourself with less disrespect and will probably feel better as a result. If you self-monitor and document your negative self-talk using this form for six weeks, it will also be a measure of your commitment and motivation to change. In cognitive trauma therapy, the clients who had the highest motivation to change and the strongest commitment to do the homework were the ones who benefited the most.

Instructions: Look at the blank self-monitoring form. Make several copies of this form. You will use one form per week. At the top of the form, put your name and the dates you will monitor yourself.

At the top of the form, notice that we list four categories of negative self-talk. Then, in the second section of the form, the days of the week are broken into time blocks. The first time in each day that you catch yourself saying or even just thinking a category 2 statement, write the number "2" in the time block when this habit occurred. For example, if you caught yourself calling yourself a "dummy" at 3 P.M. on Monday, write the number "2" in the noon to 4 P.M. block in the "Monday" column.

Please record only the first instance of a category within each time block. This method of recording is simpler and easier to do than if we asked you to record every single occurrence of negative self-talk.

In the third section of the form, there are spaces for you to write examples of your negative self-talk. Write down exactly what it is you said or thought to yourself the first time each day that you engage in each category of self-talk.

A completed self-monitoring form follows the blank form. It was completed by a woman receiving cognitive trauma therapy and reflects the woman's actual responses. Note that there are a maximum of four numbers in any time block. For example, each of the four self-talk categories occurred at least once between noon and 4 P.M. on Monday. Notice that on Saturday, negative self-talk occurred in category 3: "I feel" statements ending with words that are not emotions. In the bottom section of the form, the only statement written for Saturday is "I feel like I'm going crazy." There is no documentation of negative self-talk on Sunday.

It is extremely important that you carry this sheet around with you at all times and write down the numbers *immediately* when the self-talk occurs. If you wait until later, it defeats the purpose of the exercise. Writing down the numbers is an inconvenience or hassle and may be mildly punishing. But that's the whole idea. Mild punishment for this behavior may help break the habit. On the other hand, if you do not engage in any negative self-talk, you do not have to write anything down.

On the page following the completed self-monitoring form, there is a form for estimating your weekly total of negative self-talk for six consecutive weeks. At the end of each week, for six consecutive weeks, please record your weekly estimate of each category of negative self-talk. You will probably detect a downward trend in negative self-talk over this six-week period.

Self-Monitoring Form

Your Name: _____   Dates: from _____ to _____

Phrases of Concern:

1 = "... should ... I should have ... I could have ... Why?"

2 = Self-Put-Downs of your entire personality or character
(e.g., "I'm stupid ... I'm inadequate ... I'm a wimp," etc.)

3 = "I feel ..." statements ending with words that are not emotions
(e.g., "I feel obligated ... overwhelmed ... responsible ... sorry for ...")

4 = Apologies (i.e., "I'm sorry.")

Dates	Mon	Tues	Wed	Thurs	Fri	Sat	Sun
8 A.M. – Noon							
Noon – 4 P.M.							
4 P.M. – 8 P.M.							
8 P.M. – Midnight							
Midnight – 8 A.M.							

Monday Phrases:	1: _____ 2: _____ 3: _____
Tuesday Phrases:	1: _____ 2: _____ 3: _____
Wednesday Phrases:	1: _____ 2: _____ 3: _____
Thursday Phrases:	1: _____ 2: _____ 3: _____
Friday Phrases:	1: _____ 2: _____ 3: _____
Saturday Phrases:	1: _____ 2: _____ 3: _____
Sunday Phrases:	1: _____ 2: _____ 3: _____

Self-Monitoring Form

Your Name: _____   Dates: from _____ to _____

Phrases of Concern:

1 = ". . . should . . . I should have . . . I could have . . . Why?"

2 = Self-Put-Downs of your entire personality or character
    (e.g., "I'm stupid . . . I'm inadequate . . . I'm a wimp," etc.)

3 = "I feel . . ." statements ending with words that are not emotions
    (e.g., "I feel obligated . . . overwhelmed . . . responsible . . . sorry for . . .")

4 = Apologies (i.e., "I'm sorry.")

Dates	6/29	6/30	7/1	7/2	7/3	7/4	7/5
	Mon	**Tues**	**Wed**	**Thurs**	**Fri**	**Sat**	**Sun**
8 A.M. – Noon	1 4 3	3 4 1	1 3 2	1 2 3	1 2 3	3	
Noon – 4 P.M.	3 4 2 1	2 4 3	3 1 4	4 3 1	4 1 2		
4 P.M. – 8 P.M.	4 3 2	4 1 2 3	2 3 1	2 3 1	3 4 1		
8 P.M. – Midnight	4 3 2	3 1 2	3 2 1	3 1 2	3 4 2 1		
Midnight – 8 A.M.	1 3 2	3 2 1	3 2 1	3 2 1	3 1 2		

Monday Phrases:	1: *I could have got this ready sooner.* 2: *I am going to lose it.* 3: *I feel overwhelmed.*
Tuesday Phrases:	1: *I should have done it better.* 2: *I am so stupid.* 3: *I feel so overwhelmed.*
Wednesday Phrases:	1: *Why did I ask him for help?* 2: *I am so inadequate.* 3: *I feel overwhelmed.*
Thursday Phrases:	1: *I should have cleaned house today instead of going out.* 2: *I'm so irresponsible.* 3: *I feel overwhelmed.*
Friday Phrases:	1: *I should have put the kids' lunch together last night.* 2: *I'm a terrible mom.* 3: *I feel like I can't make it.*
Saturday Phrases:	1: _____ 2: _____ 3: *I feel like I'm going crazy.*
Sunday Phrases:	1: _____ 2: _____ 3: _____

Weekly Estimates of Negative Self-Talk (in Speech and Thoughts)

Your initials: _____

The purpose of this questionnaire is to estimate how often you engage in five categories of negative self-talk in six consecutive one-week periods. Fill in the dates for each week (e.g., from 3/19 to 3/26).

Then, record your estimate of the weekly total for each category of self-talk using this response format:

0 = Not at all   **1** = Rarely   **2** = Occasionally   **3** = Frequently   **4** = Very Frequently

Add up the weekly totals for each of the five categories and write in the weekly grand total.

	from: / to: /	from: / to: /	from: / to: /	from: / to: /	from: / to: /	from: / to: /
The word "should"—said or thought in the context of deciding what to do ("I should . . . What should I do?")						
Weekly Total:						
"I should have" or "I could have" phrases						
Weekly Total:						
"Why" questions ("Why did I . . . Why did he . . . Why me?")						
Weekly Total:						
Self-put-downs of your entire personality or character ("I'm stupid . . . a fool . . . a wimp . . . a failure . . . There's something wrong with me")						
Weekly Total:						
"I feel . . ." statements ending with words that are not pure emotions ("I feel obligated . . . I feel overwhelmed . . . I feel responsible . . . I feel sorry for . . .")						
Weekly Total:						
Weekly Grand Total:						

What If You Think Your Negative Self-Talk Is True?

Once in a great while, a client will object to giving up negative self-talk "because it's true." The point is that negative self-talk—such as, "I feel ugly," "I'm a loser," "I feel overwhelmed"—makes you feel bad and makes your symptoms worse. We occasionally illustrate this point with the following anecdote:

In the first session, a client said, "My ex-boyfriend made me feel like a worthless piece of crap." In the second session, she said, "I feel like a worthless piece of crap." Her therapist said, "You need to stop talking to yourself that way." "But it's true!" she replied. Her therapist then said, "Do you want to get over your depression and PTSD?" She said, "Of course. I wouldn't be here if I didn't want to get rid of PTSD." Then, her therapist said, "Well, you're not going to get over it if you continue to talk to yourself that way. Does calling yourself 'a worthless piece of crap' make you want to try harder or to get down on all fours and crawl away? Would calling one of your children 'stupid' or 'lazy' make her more likely to try harder or more likely to give up and stop trying?" The woman then said, "I understand. I'm going to try to stop talking to myself that way."

In our experience, many clients start to decrease their use of negative self-talk almost immediately after being given the self-monitoring homework assignment. For some clients, especially women who are not used to attending to their mental life, the habit-breaking process is slower. However, if you are strongly motivated to break bad habits of self-talk, you will be able to do it by paying close attention to your mental life and documenting occurrences of negative self-talk on the self-monitoring form.

Chapter Follow-Up

Write down the day and date that is exactly fourteen days from today: _____ .
Mark that date on your calendar and bookmark this page. Fourteen days from now, come back to this place in the workbook and answer the following question:

What have you learned from engaging in the self-monitoring exercises?

_____

_____

_____

_____

CHAPTER 5

The Power of Nonnegative Thinking

In this chapter you will learn much more about the power of negative self-talk. Negative self-talk is like a cancer, and the more you realize how personally harmful it is, the more strongly motivated you will be to break these habits. And the more strongly motivated you are, the more quickly these terrible habits will be broken.

In chapter 4, you learned how to monitor or keep track of four categories of self-talk (in your speech and thoughts), which encompass almost all the ways you can talk disrespectfully to yourself. We are going to discuss three of these categories in greater depth. We'll also discuss some alternatives.

Category 1: "Should," "Should Have," "Could Have," and "Why?"

What does it mean to say, "I *should* do something"? It means that you're *obligated* to do something. You're *supposed to* do something. You *have to* do something. Unfortunately, women are taught as children many "supposed to" beliefs that lead them to believe they are supposed to do all kinds of things that are not a good idea and only maintain the existing social order of male dominance and female subordination. Hence, shoulds are "supposed tos"—but it may or may not be in your best interests to do what you think you should do. For example, you may have asked yourself, "Should I give him another chance? Should I stay? I guess I should. After all, he apologized, and I'm supposed to be a forgiving person. And marriage is *supposed* to be forever, after all. I should stand by my man . . . On the other hand, is it a good idea to forgive him and act like it never happened? I don't know. But, I should. I'm supposed to."

When trying to decide what to do, ask yourself instead: "What course of action is most likely to be in my best interests? What course of action is most likely to promote my long-term happiness? What good things and bad things are likely to happen if I do this? What good things and bad things are likely to happen if I do something else?"

In other words, when you are tempted to say "I wonder what I should do?" rephrase the question! Millions of women would have ended an abusive relationship sooner or would have been less likely to have gone back after leaving had they made their decisions based on an intellectual analysis of the likely consequences of leaving or staying—rather than on the basis of some irrational "should." In summary, the word *should* is an undesirable word and you do not need to use this word to communicate or make decisions effectively.

Three Good Reasons

The phrases *should have* and *could have* are not good for you for at least three reasons. First, statements that include the phrases *should have* or *could have* usually signal the presence of guilt, and guilt, of course, is a source of emotional pain. But, it's worse than that because when you say, "I should have" or "I could have," it usually signals guilt that has no rational basis. You are usually making a thinking error that causes you to draw a faulty conclusion about your role in a negative event. When you say (or think) the phrase *should have* or *could have,* you are falsely remembering an unforeseeable negative outcome as foreseeable, which leads straight to guilt. This tendency to remember unforeseeable outcomes as foreseeable is called *hindsight bias.* We will have more to tell you about hindsight bias in chapter 10.

A second reason why the phrases *should have* and *could have* are not good for you is that they make you feel bad. Saying "I should have" or "I could have" is self-criticism or self-punishment that makes you feel bad and lowers your self-esteem. What if a friend or relative said to you, "You could have prevented the abuse," or "You shouldn't have married him," or "You should put it behind you and get on with your life," or "You shouldn't feel that way"? Would you feel better? Of course not! You wouldn't feel better because it's criticism, and criticism doesn't feel good. These words have the same negative effect when you say them to yourself.

A third reason why the phrases *should have* and *could have* are not good for you is that they are often followed by or lead to the second category of negative self-talk—shame-related put-downs of your entire personality, character, or intelligence. And put-downs of your entire self can be even more painful than saying or thinking, "I should have" or "I could have." The bottom line is, you need to give yourself the same kind of respect that you would like to get from other people.

What about "Why"?

Now, we are going to elaborate on reasons why "why" questions are not good for you. One reason is that *why* questions often lead to "should have" statements and guilt. For example, when you ask, "Why did I do (something)?" you will often then say or think, "I shouldn't have done that." Do you see how "should have" statements often follow from *why* questions? Similarly, *why* questions can also give rise to anger. Here are two examples: "Why did he do that? He shouldn't have done that! . . . Why did the criminal justice system fail me? It's unfair. I shouldn't have been treated unfairly by the system!"

When it comes to anger, spending your time on the things you can't change is an opportunity lost in terms of time you could spend on improving your life. That's one of the reasons we are going to help you stop asking "why" questions that lead to anger. Asking why does you no good at all! The next time you ask why, quickly ask yourself a "what" question: "What am I going to do about it?" If your answer is "nothing," change the subject. You are wasting your time.

The third set of statements on the self-advocacy questionnaire from chapter 2 is pertinent here: "It does not promote my long-term happiness to think or talk about things that I cannot change—such as dwelling on the unfairness of the system or past injustices. The time I spend on such things is time I cannot spend working on things I can control, change, or do something about. Time spent doing things of little value costs me the opportunity of spending that time doing something that is more worthwhile. In other words, spending time on things I can't change does not belong on my daily to do list!"

Another problem with *why* questions is that they can keep you stuck in the past. There is no problem solving involved because knowing why is not going to change what happened. It just keeps you stuck in pain, something like helpless anger or helpless rage. You're wanting to control or undo something that you cannot control or change.

You may think that if you found the answer, you would feel better. This is almost always not true: "Why was he so brutal and cruel? Why would someone—who said he loved me more than he ever loved anyone—treat me that way? . . . Why did he keep lying to me? . . . Why did he cheat on me? . . . Why didn't he realize that he was destroying my love for him?"

Knowing the answers will not change that fact that you were betrayed. Knowing why will not undo what happened. Knowing why will not enable this woman to change this guy into a loving, caring, faithful, and compassionate husband. It is usually a fantasy when you think, "If I just find out why, I'll feel better."

Category 2: Shame-Related Put-Downs of Your Personality, Character, or Intelligence

We are going to talk only briefly about put-downs of your entire self because it is so obvious that this kind of self-talk does nothing but drag you down and keep you down.

Such expressions as "I feel stupid . . . I'm inadequate . . . I'm an emotional mess . . . I'm a wimp . . . There's something wrong with me . . . I feel ashamed" are all expressions of shame. *Shame* is defined as an unpleasant feeling plus a negative evaluation of your entire self, personality, intelligence, or character—often expressed as an "I feel . . ." statement (Kubany and Watson 2003). Talking negatively about yourself in shaming ways not only makes you feel bad, it also lowers your self-esteem. Why would anyone want to lower her self-esteem?

Expressions of Shame

There are almost an infinite variety of ways that you could verbally communicate the experience of shame. The following is a collection of examples of ways that our clients have verbally communicated shame during therapy sessions (Kubany and Watson 2003).

Would putting yourself down these ways make you want to try harder or make you want to get down on all fours and crawl away? Again, you need to start giving yourself the same kind of respect you would like to get—and deserve to get—from other people.

I feel like I'm a nobody.

I'm feeling no self-worth.

There's something wrong with me.

I feel so dirty and ugly.

I'm ashamed of my whole life.

I was so stupid . . . an idiot.

I'm damaged goods.

I'm an emotional mess.

I feel scarred for life.

I feel like a dysfunctional person.

I hate myself.

I feel like a child.

I feel like a failure.

I feel unqualified.

I feel mortified and humiliated.

I feel selfish.

I feel like an outcast.

I feel incompetent.

I'm a bad mother.

I'm such a fool.

I feel like I'm always wrong.

I feel so beaten down and defeated.

I'm not lovable.

I'm not good enough.

I feel like a tramp.

I feel like a horrible person.

I feel like a total loser.

I don't feel normal.

I'm disgusted with myself.

I'm a wimp . . . pathetic.

Category 3: "I Feel" Sentences That End with Words That Are Not Emotions

How you feel is extremely important—obviously—and communicating to others how you feel is very, very important too. However, it is equally important that you only use the phrase "I feel" when communicating emotional experiences, which are relatively pure feelings. There are only a small number of relatively pure feelings. These relatively pure feelings are vague, diffuse, positive or negative emotions that do not have much content or meaning attached. You can be in a good mood or bad mood regardless of what is going on around you. You can wake up in the morning and feel anxious or sad or be in a bad mood or feel yucky or down even if you have every reason to be in a good mood. It's just a bad biorhythm day. Or, you can be in a good mood even though you have reasons to be in a bad mood. We have all had days like these.

Here's a list of relatively pure negative emotions:

- distress

- upset

- hurt

- sadness

- frustration

- disappointment

- fear

- anxiety

- unhappiness

- emotional pain

Hybrid Emotions

All other emotional experiences are combinations of the pure emotions and certain kinds of appraisals, interpretations, or attributions. We call these emotional experiences *hybrid emotions*. The following are hybrid negative emotions:

- guilt

- anger

- resentment

- shame

- regret

Read the list out loud.

The word *hybrid* comes from genetics research. You can cross two different fruits—like oranges and tangerines—and get a tangelo, a new fruit, that's a hybrid.

Similarly, by crossing thoughts and feelings, you get hybrid emotions. They have a thinking part and a feeling part.

What is the relatively pure negative feeling that you have when you experience guilt?

_____

Some type of distress, right? Perhaps emotional upset, emotional pain, or just a yucky feeling. And what thoughts run through your mind when you experience guilt?

_____

Did you write "I should have done something differently . . . I screwed up . . . It's my fault"? Do you point a negative finger at yourself for acting in a certain way?

We could just as easily ask you, "What do you *think* guilty about?" as "What do you *feel* guilty about?" because guilt has a thinking component as well as a feeling component. It would be most accurate to say, "I *experience* guilt," which acknowledges that guilt is a combination of feelings and thoughts. The same holds true for other hybrid emotions, like anger and shame.

How to Think Clearly

Some therapists think it is their job to help clients sort out their feelings. We think it is our job to help clients think more clearly. We also believe that people can only have one emotional experience at a time—although different emotional experiences can follow one another in rapid succession. For example, consider the following sequence of statements made by a Vietnam veteran: "I never should have fired into that village. I should have known there were women and children there and that the enemy was long gone. I'm a horrible person for firing on that village. That damn lieutenant. He never should have told us to fire at that village."

Or consider this series of statements: "I never should have married him. I should have seen the signs. What an idiot. I was so stupid. But why did he deceive and manipulate me? He never should have done that. That jerk!"

The Vietnam vet and the formerly battered woman both feel guilt, shame, and anger—the same negative feelings—but their emotional experiences are different because they are thinking about different things.

How to Determine the Validity of an Idea or Opinion

Read aloud the following list of words:

- responsible

- obligated

- overwhelmed

- unsafe

- abandoned

- helpless

- dirty

- mistrustful

- wrong

- stuck

- weak

- strong

These words are *not* emotions. They are ideas, intellectual judgments, beliefs, opinions, or conclusions about fact that can only be determined to be true or false based on evidence or proof. We know these ideas are true or not based on factual evidence—not feelings.

Consider the word *responsible*. To conclude that someone is responsible means that this person has caused something to happen. Whether a person is responsible or not can only be determined based on evidence. Do you think a judge wants the jury to say how they *feel* about the defendant?

The judge wants the jury to weigh the evidence to determine whether the defendant was responsible for causing the crime.

Now look at the word *obligated*. An obligation is a debt. If you charge something on your charge card, you are obligated to restore the balance. If you hire someone to clean your apartment, you are obligated to pay them. An obligation means that a person has a moral duty to do something. Whether someone is truly obligated in a situations requires analysis of the facts.

Next, consider the word *overwhelmed*. To say someone is overwhelmed means that this person is totally overpowered and completely helpless—completely powerless to prevent something bad from happening. Only slaves, prisoners, children, and victims of abuse are overwhelmed. This isn't an emotion. It is a cold, hard fact.

Finally, consider the word *unsafe*. Your home or apartment may be safe or unsafe from intruders. Does your home have locks on the doors and windows? Do you have a smoke alarm? Do you have a security alarm? Do you have a security guard? Are you living with someone who could protect you? Do you have neighbors you can trust? Do police patrol the area on a regular basis? Do you live in a safe neighborhood, where there is very little crime? Whether your home is a relatively safe or unsafe place to live can only be determined based on an analysis of factual evidence. Safety can only be evaluated on the basis of the facts. The state of being safe is not a feeling, is it?

Emotional Reasoning

Now read aloud the following statements:

- I feel responsible.

- I feel obligated.

- I feel overwhelmed.

- I don't feel safe.

- I feel abandoned.

- I feel helpless.

- I feel dirty.

- I don't feel I can trust.

- I always feel wrong.

- I feel stuck in a hole.

- I feel weak.

- I feel strong.

Do these sound like statements of emotion? Are they?

Just because you said "I feel" with these words does not make them emotions, does it? In addition, the feelings that accompany these words are not evidence for the truth, accuracy, or validity of the conclusions that these ideas convey. Using feelings associated with an idea as evidence for the truth of an idea is called *emotional reasoning*.

Emotional reasoning could also be called "lazy thinking," because when you say "I feel" with words that are not emotions, you don't challenge the conclusions. You just accept the conclusions as true—without looking at evidence as to whether or to what degree they are true. You just assume the conclusions are true. We call it "lazy thinking" when our clients do not think critically and do not question or challenge their reasons for believing what they believe.

Carole's Story

Carole said, "I feel I abandoned my children." Her therapist asked her what she did that constituted abandonment of her children. Carole said that she had been planning to leave an abusive marriage, so she decided to get a job to make it easier for her to support her children and become independent enough to leave her husband. Unfortunately, there were no jobs in the small town where they lived, so Carole moved temporarily to Dallas, where work was available. As it unforeseeably turned out, Carole did not get her kids back for several years. Would you conclude that Carole abandoned her children?

Carole uncritically accepted the conclusion that she had abandoned her children simply because she felt she had abandoned them. She did not challenge the conclusion or weigh the evidence to see if her conclusion made sense. This was lazy thinking.

Dr. Kubany first became interested in "I feel" language when he started helping clients analyze their guilt issues in 1990. At the end of a session, clients would often say something like, "I see where you're going with this and, intellectually it makes sense. But, I still feel responsible." By saying "I feel responsible," you are using your feelings as evidence for a conclusion that you are responsible. Somehow, "I feel responsible" seems more true than, "I think I'm responsible." Adding the words "I feel" gives the conclusion a false ring of truth. It makes the idea expressed *feel* more true.

Similarly, consider the statement "I feel obligated." Many battered women say they feel obligated to stay (or reconcile) with their abusers in spite of repeated abuse. Did you ever feel obligated to your abuser? Yes _____ No _____ . If yes, in what way(s) did you feel obligated to him?

_____

What is the evidence that you were obligated in this way or these ways?

_____

What is the evidence that you were not obligated?

_____

Well, if you were obligated to your abuser, it must mean that he was doing all the giving, and you were doing all the taking. Therefore, you had an obligation to return the favor, or pay him back in some way to restore the balance. Is that the way it was? Not likely.

Learned Helplessness

Consider the phrase "I feel overwhelmed." This kind of statement reflects *learned helplessness* (see chapter 8). Learned helplessness or learned powerlessness is the persistent learned belief that you are powerless to prevent bad things from happening and the associated belief that it makes no sense to even try to escape from intolerably bad situations—even when you are no longer helpless or powerless. In other words, learned powerlessness is the belief that you have no options available to stop bad things from happening—when options do in fact exist and you are not powerless. The phrase "I feel overwhelmed" is one of many statements ingrained in the vocabulary of battered and formerly battered women who, because of their experiences of victimization, think they have no power or options for solving their problems.

"I feel overwhelmed" tops the list of learned powerlessness statements made by formerly battered women. Other "I feel" statements that reflect perceived powerlessness include "I feel trapped . . . I feel cornered . . . I feel stuck . . . I feel stuck in a hole . . . I feel helpless . . . I feel out of control . . . I feel like I'm suffocating . . . I feel like there's a pillow over my head . . . I feel like my back's against the wall . . . I feel like I'm going to be cut to shreds . . . I feel like I have to . . . I feel like I'm walking on eggshells . . . I feel like I'm under a tidal wave . . . I feel like I'm on a high wire without a net below . . . I feel like I've run out of options."

Sound familiar?

What is the evidence that *you* have no options? Like everyone else, you can't do everything; therefore, you need to prioritize. If you feel overwhelmed, how do you think the president of the United States feels? He probably doesn't feel overwhelmed. He knows he can't do everything, but he also knows he needs to prioritize and do the most important things he has to do in the time available. He has a lot to do, but he is not without options—and neither are you without options.

Are You Safe or Not?

Now consider the statements "I don't feel safe" and "I feel safe." If you don't feel safe, it does not mean that you are unsafe. Similarly, if you feel safe, it does not mean that you are safe. One of the things that shelter workers shudder to hear a battered woman say is something like this: "He apologized. He agreed to go to anger management. He never agreed to go to anger management before. Maybe I should go back. I think I will. After all, I *feel* safe."

Is her conclusion that she feels safe evidence that she is safe? In the example above, this woman's husband has apologized countless times, and this is her third time at the shelter. Based on the evidence, is this woman safe?

Elizabeth's Story

Elizabeth went to a support group but didn't go back because she didn't like hearing the other women talk about incidents of abuse. But Elizabeth did get one thing out of the group—the emphasis on safety. Unfortunately, she translated this emphasis on safety to mean that anything that made her feel safe was a good idea. And that anything that made her feel unsafe should be a signal to take action. Elizabeth's abusive ex-boyfriend had broken into her apartment one time some three years earlier. It was the middle of the night. Therefore, ever since she went to the support group, Elizabeth has tried to sleep during the day—when she felt safe—and to stay awake at night—when she felt unsafe. Did this make any sense?

Elizabeth also engaged in a ritual done by a surprising number of formerly battered women. When she would get home from work, she would immediately look under the bed (and get relief reinforcement), look in the closet (getting a couple of seconds of relief), and then look behind the shower curtain (and get relief again). But Elizabeth also did something that was even more extreme than this. After she was home for a while, she would have a gut feeling that her ex-boyfriend was in the bedroom, so she would go look in the bedroom. A while later, Elizabeth might have a feeling that her abuser was in the kitchen, so she would go look in the kitchen.

Elizabeth had a twelve-year-old daughter, and she was afraid that her ex-boyfriend might try to kidnap her, even though she had no evidence that he might do this. When Elizabeth dropped her daughter off at school, she would sometimes have a feeling that her abuser was lurking nearby, so she would drive around the block for reassurance (relief) that he wasn't there. Sometimes, Elizabeth would have a feeling that she had just missed him, so she would drive around the block again. Her therapist said to this, "Why stop at twice? Why not three or four times? Why not circle the perimeter until she gets out of school?"

Elizabeth would also spend about ten minutes driving around the parking lot at Safeway because she had a feeling he might be there. Was this a good use of her time? Did her behavior make any sense at all?

Safety Is Not a Feeling

Two women who participated in our therapy program lived in the same boarding house. One of these women didn't feel safe with her room unlocked. The other woman didn't feel safe with her door locked. Now, ordinarily you might think that the women would be safer with the doors locked—unless perhaps, you knew the history of this boarding house. It had had three fires in the past two years because of faulty wiring. But neither of these women were looking at whether their conclusions had any basis in objective evidence. They were more concerned about feeling safe, which had more to do with past experience than with the present facts. What bad thing do you think happened in the past to the woman who didn't feel safe with the door unlocked? What bad thing do you think happened to the other woman?

In the first case, the woman had been sexually assaulted by a man who walked into her apartment through an unlocked door.

The other woman had been severely beaten as she tried to get out of her apartment but couldn't escape because the door was locked.

Upon hearing this story, another client said, "I do that. I don't lock my car doors. In fact, I don't lock my house doors, either." It turned out that this woman had been assaulted and nearly killed by her boyfriend in his locked pickup truck. This woman did not have the slightest idea why she was not locking her doors—and actually jeopardizing her safety—other than the fact that she felt safer with unlocked doors. Her ability to think clearly and logically was impaired by her reliance on emotional reasoning.

The Importance of Being Rational

Research has shown that if we induce negative emotions in people—for example, make them feel anxious or angry—they tend to make self-defeating decisions (Leith and Baumeister 1996). Bad moods interfere with your ability to think clearly and make decisions that are in your best interests. When people are in bad moods, they tend to make decisions based on what they think will make them feel better immediately rather than on an analysis of what is in their long-term best interests. We will give you an example to illustrate.

Joan's Story

A thirty-year-old Hawaiian woman was taking part in a study to assess participants' prior exposure to traumatic life events and their after-effects. Joan had been horribly abused—both physically and psychologically—by her first husband when she was in her early twenties. Now, Joan was remarried to someone who was not physically abusive but who was extremely controlling and even more psychologically abusive than her first husband. Joan was extremely unhappy and suffering from severe PTSD. As part of the debriefing process, the psychologist-assessor engaged Joan in a decision-making exercise: she asked Joan to identify the likely short-term and long-term positive consequences and negative consequences of two courses of action—staying with her second husband or returning to her family on the mainland with her two small children. Anyone who looked at this woman's responses on this exercise would see that her only hope of any future happiness would be to leave her husband. At the end of the exercise, the psychologist asked Joan what she was going to do. She only said, "If I leave him, I'll feel like I'm abandoning him."

Decisions that lead to relief from negative feelings are usually not logical. This is an important reason why major decisions should never be made in high states of emotion. Here's a sample of the logic of many battered women: "I feel sorry for him. He misses me. He's falling apart at the seams. He says he'll never do it again. I feel sorry for him. Maybe I should go back. You know, I'll probably feel better if I go back. I'm going to give him another chance."

It would be much better to ask, "What's in my best interests? What is likely to happen in the short term if I go back?" ("Well, I'll probably experience less guilt.") "What if he hits me again in front of the children?" ("Oh, my gosh! Then I'll feel guilty because I went back!")

Doing something to get rid of guilt is no guarantee that you are going to be free of guilt. Decisions that are driven by emotional impulses are virtually never in your best interests.

Strong Motivation Is a Prerequisite for Breaking Any Persistent Bad Habit

In cognitive trauma therapy, most clients are engaging in less and less negative self-talk within three or four weeks after starting to monitor their negative self-talk. Once in a while, however, a client will still be engaging in a great deal of negative self-talk after several weeks of self-monitoring. And when negative self-talk stays at a high level, PTSD symptoms almost always also remain at moderate to high levels. We have found that the problem in such cases is that these women are not sufficiently motivated to break these self-talk habits—it doesn't bother them enough, so they continue to engage in the habit. For example, the therapist might say, "Did you hear what you just said? You just did it again. You just said, 'I'm stupid' and went right on talking." And the client says, "I know. I've been beating myself up all day." The therapist might then say something like, "What we mean by strong motivation to break these habits is something like this: 'I did it again! Darn. How frustrating. I'm going to break these habits if it's the last thing I do. I *know* it's not good for me!'"

We have found that it sometimes takes a pep talk like this to sufficiently increase a woman's commitment and determination to enable her to break negative self-talk habits.

Are you more motivated now than ever to stop using negative self-talk and to break these habits?

What did you learn from reading this chapter and answering the questions?

CHAPTER 6

Managing Stress by Controlling Muscle Tension

A major goal of this book is to empower you. Being empowered involves being able to control how you feel and having confidence in your skills to handle difficult and potentially stressful situations. In chapter 4, you learned a way to control how you feel by the way that you talk to yourself—the ticker tape of thoughts that continuously run through your mind. We pointed out that if you are not aware of your negative self-talk scripts or how they drag you down, you are out of control. You are not in control of your well-being. In this chapter, you will learn another way to control how you feel. You can control your emotional well-being by controlling the tension in your muscles. Muscles are always tense when you experience fear, anxiety, frustration, anger, and even depression. But, when muscles are relaxed, the mind is relaxed.

In this chapter, you will learn that there is a very strong relationship or connection between physical tension and emotional distress. In talking to you about stress and how to regulate stress, we will emphasize and reemphasize the importance of keeping the tension in your body at a low level. We will discuss six different reasons why it is important to keep your general level of tension low. Easier said then done, of course, but we will teach you practical skills that you can employ on a daily basis to regulate your levels of physiological arousal—and in so doing regulate your moods and emotional well-being.

The Meaning of Stress

What is stress? Describe what stress means to you.

_____

_____

_____

_____

Did you mention some external event that causes you stress or distress? Something outside of yourself that is acting on you or happening to you? In stress, there is usually an external stimulus from the environment exerting some kind of pressure on you—somebody wanting you to do something, someone criticizing you, something you have to do, a deadline you need to meet, or an interruption (for example, your kids making demands when you are trying to concentrate).

In your description of stress, did you refer to something negative happening inside of you as well? Stress always includes an internal reaction in response to an outside stimulus—anxiety, tension, sweaty palms, a headache. Negative events not only have psychological effects; they also affect the body and have physical effects.

Your interpretation of a negative stimulus can affect the magnitude or intensity of your internal response (for example, "feeling overwhelmed," "more than I can handle," "spread too thin"). Your interpretation of potentially stressful events can have a big influence on your internal reaction. Your brain is a cognitive filter that gives the event meaning and can help to explain why something that is a big deal to you is not a big deal to someone else. For example, research on assertiveness has shown that assertive women tend to interpret a socially stressful situation as challenging, whereas unassertive women tend to interpret the same situation as threatening (Tomaka et al. 1999, p. 1008). As a consequence, socially stressful situations cause more anxiety and more negative physical reactions in unassertive women than in assertive women. As another example, because of their history of abuse, formerly battered women with PTSD tend to interpret disagreements and raised voices much more negatively than women who do not have histories of abuse. As a result, arguments and disagreements are much more stressful for these women than for women who have never been abused.

Stress is the negative emotional reaction you have in response to negative events. In other words, stress is your body's reaction of physical arousal in response to external demands. When scientists first started investigating stress, they were studying physical reactions in response to actual *physical* pressures, such as blood pressure or water pressure. Hans Selye, the scientist who coined the term stress, studied the adaptation of laboratory animals in response to prolonged physical stressors, such as cold, heat, and low-grade shock (Selye 1956). When most people think of stress today, however, they are usually referring to emotional reactions that are triggered by psychological or social events that do not have any direct or obvious immediate physical impact or physical effects. For example, "pressure" from other people usually comes in the form of spoken words, not fists or baseball bats.

Stress as Change

Another way to look at stress is in terms of change. Any change in the flow of life events is an interruption that requires or calls for some adaptation or adjustment. Change itself, and the process of getting used to change, tend to be stressful. Some examples include losing a job, having to move, getting a divorce, a parent getting cancer, or experiencing any traumatic event. Some research has shown a correlation between the number of major life changes a person has experienced in the past year and the amount of recent illness the person has had. Still another way to look at stress as change is in terms of the mini-changes that occur for everyone every day. For example, the alarm doesn't go off; you're out of milk; one of the children is crying or the kids are arguing with one another; you can't find something; you're stuck in traffic; you forgot something at home; someone at work is complaining; you get a phone call from your abuser.

Exercise: Everyday Mini-Stresses

What are some of the mini-stresses that happened to you today?" (If you can't think of at least three examples, go back to yesterday and include mini-stresses that happened yesterday.)

1. _____

2. _____

3. _____

4. _____

Even though any one of the mini-stresses you identified may have been relatively minor, can you see how their effects can sometimes build up?

Stress Tends to Accumulate

Many people do not realize that stress tends to build or accumulate. When you experience a stressor or stressful event, your tension level goes up. After the stressor is removed, your level of tension goes down—but it doesn't go down all the way. Interruptions in the flow of the day lead to a gradually increasing level of physical tension. For example, you wake up late. Your tension goes up because you're late, and then it goes back down—but not all the way. You're out of milk. Your tension goes up, and then it goes back down—but not to where it was before you noticed you were out of milk. You're stuck on the freeway. Your tension goes up, and then it goes back down—but not to where it was before. You realize you forgot something at home. Your tension goes up, and then it goes back down—but not to where it was before you realized you'd forgotten something. After each stressor, your body holds on to a little more tension. Can you see how the day can start out great, and by 4 P.M., you're a nervous wreck? Have you had days like this one? Everyone has them. But some people have worse days than others. And people with PTSD have worse days than people who don't have PTSD.

The Relationship between Mental Activity and Physical Activity

When you are stressed mentally, your body reacts in a variety of ways—for example, by increases in heart rate, blood pressure, sweat gland activity, muscle tension, and secretions of hormones. If someone says that her stress is strictly in her mind—in between her ears—she is not aware of how her body is reacting. For example, if a person says she is psychologically upset but physically relaxed, she is not aware of the physical changes that are occurring in her body. There is an extremely strong correlation between mental activity and physical activity—between the mind and the body—between mental distress and physical distress. There are a variety of ways that people experience stress or emotional distress, which is always associated with elevations in physical arousal. Anxiety, fear, panic, bad moods, and depression are all associated with elevations in physical or physiological arousal.

Muscle Tension and Negative Emotional States

By calming your body, you can calm your mind and gain control over your moods. States of mental tranquility and mental peace are associated with decreases in physiological arousal. As we said earlier, one of the major objectives of this chapter is to give you tools for alleviating stress by calming your body. You are going to alleviate your stress by learning a general method of relaxation and applying this method after experiencing stress.

Muscle Tension Is Not Synonymous with Negative Emotion

We recommend muscle relaxation as a vehicle or tool for improving your emotional well-being and for alleviating stress. However, muscle tension itself is not the same as anxiety, fear, anger, or other states of negative emotion. You can have tense muscles and still be very relaxed. However, when you are in a state of fear, anger, or depression, your muscles are always tense. Have you ever seen a cat who was angry or afraid who had relaxed muscles? It's not possible, is it? It's the same with people.

If Your Muscles Are Completely Relaxed, You Cannot Be Depressed, Angry, or Afraid

By relaxing your muscles, other physiological reactions associated with fear, anger, frustration, or depression also decrease. For example, as your muscles relax, your heart rate goes down, your blood pressure goes down, you perspire less, and you secrete fewer hormones. If your muscles are relaxed, your heart can't race, and you can't hyperventilate. It's physiologically impossible. In fact, complete relaxation is associated with a positive sense of well-being. By controlling the tension in your muscles, you can control your mood and your mind.

A prerequisite to relaxation is body awareness. If you are not aware of where your body is reacting when you are experience stress, you are not in direct control of your emotional well-being. In addition to monitoring your negative self-talk, we want you to become a very accurate observer of your body. We want you to become very aware of where you experience muscle tension and how tense or relaxed your muscles are.

The Importance of Keeping Your Tension Level Low

There are at least six reasons you want to try to keep your general level of tension at a low level.

1. The first reason you want to keep your tension level low is that it is easier to identify increases in muscle tension at low levels than at high levels. You are only in a position to do something to decrease the tension in your body if you know where that tension is. If you are unaware of where your body reacts when you experience stress, you can't do anything about it, and you are not in control.

2. The second reason that you want to keep your tension at low levels is that it is easier to relax or bring your level of tension down when your tension is relatively low than when your tension level is high. For example, it is easier to go from a tension score of 30 to 20 than from a tension score of 70 to 60 (where 100 is the highest and 0 is the lowest level of tension).

3. A third reason you want to keep your tension at a low level is that high levels of tension impair your ability to think clearly. In particular, the ability to make important decisions that are in your best interests is impaired when your tension level is high.

4. The fourth reason you want to keep your tension level low is that bad habits are more likely to be activated when your tension level is high. For example, when you are stressed, you are more likely to engage in negative self-talk than when you are relaxed or calm. At times when you need to be your own strongest advocate, you may be your own worst enemy.

5. The fifth reason you want to keep your tension level low is that chronically high tension or chronic hyperarousal can weaken you physically, thereby heightening vulnerability to disease and contributing to poor health. Individuals who have endured traumatic events, particularly those with PTSD, are at heightened risk for problems with physical health—including complaints of poor health status, a variety of somatic symptoms, and several diseases with a medical explanation, such as arthritis and diabetes (Golding 1994). Chronic physiological arousal may be an important contributing factor. For example, there is some evidence that individuals with PTSD have higher resting heart rates and blood pressures than individuals without PTSD (Muraoka, Carlson, and Chemtob 1998).

6. The sixth reason you want to keep the level of muscle tension in your body at a low level is you are more vulnerable to losing control—panicking, losing your temper, breaking down—in response to some stressful event if your tension level is high. Everyone has a tension level at which they will lose control—a point at which they will break down, panic, lose their temper, or otherwise lose their composure. The key is to keep your tension level nowhere near that point. Let's say the point at which you lose control is a tension score of 80. If you're having a really bad day and hovering around 70 or so, it is not going to take much to push you over the top.

   Many battered women feel guilty about losing their temper with their children over "little things." Imagine that a young child comes up to her mother, who is in a high state of tension, and pokes her in the back, calling "Mommy, Mommy!" And the mother loses her temper and yells at her child. Later, the mother may be thinking, "Why did I overreact? Why did I lose my temper over such a little thing?" Well, if you're near your "lose it" threshold, it's not going to take much to push you over the top. If you are at a low level of tension, you are far less likely to lose control in response to any kind of stressful event than if your tension level is high.

   Look at the graph below. What this figure shows is that as your level of arousal or activation increases, your level of functioning will also increase—up to a point. For example, some people seem to need that first cup of coffee in the morning before they can start getting anything done. The caffeine is a stimulant that heightens arousal. With no energy, you may not even want to get out of bed. As arousal increases, your performance increases up to the point that your level of functioning is optimal. Once arousal increases past a certain point, however, performance or level of functioning starts to deteriorate or decline. This is a problem for many people who have PTSD. Look at the downward arrow on the right side of the figure. This is where people with PTSD are most of the time. It's like they've already had three cups of coffee when they get up in the morning. They are overaroused and, as a result, they have problems with concentration. And the more aroused they get, the poorer they function.

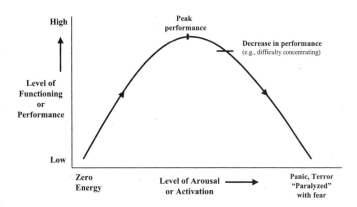

When women are trapped in an abusive relationship, they may be so upset that their ability to think rationally is severely impaired. Their tension is so high that they seem to be in a chronic state of confusion, unable to sort things out or make rational decisions. A good example of this involved a very bright woman with an advanced degree in mental health who thought she should have left her abusive boyfriend sooner. When asked when she should have left, she described a time when her boyfriend had become extremely controlling. For example, if he wanted to go to bed, he insisted that she go to bed too. At these times, she would often lie awake until he fell asleep. Then, she would go into the living room, get into a fetal position on the floor, and she would rock. Do you think this women was in any position to logically weigh the pros and cons about whether to stay or leave the relationship?

PTSD and Stress

We will illustrate how chronic PTSD arousal may contribute to disease by briefly describing the work of Hans Selye, the scientist who coined the word *stress* (Selye 1956). Selye investigated the body's response to prolonged, physically stressful events. For example, he exposed laboratory animals to prolonged cold. The animals' initial bodily reaction was one of heightened arousal to combat the "threat," and then arousal continued to remain elevated to provide resistance or ability to cope with the cold. Imagine yourself falling into cold water. At first you will start shivering and experience the intense pain of the cold. After a while, however, you will feel less cold as your body's heightened arousal provides you some resistance or protection. If the cold continues, however, the body's resources eventually become depleted. In the case of Selye's lab animals, they eventually collapsed from exhaustion and got sick or developed disease.

What happened to you may be analogous to what happened to the animals in Selye's experiments—with one very important difference. To combat the abuse from your partner, you developed PTSD, and the associated heightened arousal may have helped you endure or cope with the abuse. However, in PTSD, the heightened arousal does not go back to baseline levels after the trauma is over and you are safe. That's why they call it "post" or after the trauma stress disorder. For whatever reason, heightened arousal persists even when heightened arousal is no longer adaptive or helpful. Even though you may be safely out of an abusive relationship, your levels of physiological arousal may still be elevated, and this may be putting you at risk for disease. Consider the following analogy. Let's say you are driving around town, and when you return home, you park your car but do not turn off the ignition. You leave your car running until you want to use it again. Obviously, your car will wear out more quickly if you don't turn it off than if you turn the engine off whenever you are not using the car. In a similar way, your body may be wearing out more quickly if it is in a chronic state of high tension or hyperarousal. This is a very important reason to bring your tension level down and keep it at a low level.

Two Ways of Lowering Tension

There are two general ways to lower tension and regulate your stress in the long run. The first general way of regulating stress in the long run is to get less and less stressed or bothered when exposed to the same kinds of stressors. You need to get to the point where certain kinds of stressors bother you less and less (for example, get to the point of letting traffic on the freeway bother you less and less). The way to achieve this is through exposure and practice.

The second general way of regulating stress is to learn to recover more and more quickly when the stressor is removed. How can you keep recurring stressful events (deadlines or hassles at work; the kids' misbehaving; phone calls from your abuser) from ruining your day? How can you keep recurring stressful events from ruining your afternoon? How can you keep these events from ruining your lunch hour?

The first goal is to become less and less bothered by habitual stressful events in your life. The second goal is to get your tension back to a low level more and more quickly after stressful events have ended.

As you work on these goals, it is important that you think of your progress in reducing your general levels of stress in terms of a trend. How can you make this week better than last week? How can you make this month better than last month? How can you make this year better than last year? Remember, a lapse is not a relapse. For example, a bad day does not signify a bad month. Think in terms of the big picture.

Progressive Muscle Relaxation

Now, you are going to learn how to relax with a method called *progressive muscle relaxation*. This method of relaxation was developed by a psychologist named Edmund Jacobson, who lived well into his nineties. Some people think he may have lived for so long because he learned to relax so deeply and didn't stress his body. Originally, Dr. Jacobson thought it would take a long time for a person to learn how to relax completely—as with something like yoga or transcendental meditation. But he found out that most people can learn how to relax in a relatively short period of time; and with practice they can relax more and more quickly.

A Brief Relaxation Exercise

This technique for relaxing involves a sequential tensing and releasing of muscles. Read the four-step instructions below before you engage in the exercise. After you have read these instructions and understand clearly what they are asking you to do, perform this exercise and observe your body carefully as you do.

1. Get yourself into a comfortable position in an armchair or, if you wish, lie down on your couch or bed.

2. Clench your right fist really tight. Now hold the tension at a peak for at least five to ten seconds.

3. As you are doing step number 2, point with your left hand to where you feel the tension.

4. After clenching for five to ten seconds, unclench your fist. Get your arm into a comfortable position and just concentrate on letting go. Keep letting go.

As you were clenching your fist, did you point to your right forearm? Your forearm is the primary locus or center of tension when you clench your fist. You also may have noticed some tension in your right fist.

When you stopped clenching your fist, did you notice letting-go or draining-out sensations? When you clenched your fist and tensed up, you became more tense than you were before you clenched. But, when you stopped clenching your fist and kept letting go, you became more relaxed in your arm than you were initially. This letting go involves your muscles releasing tension.

This letting-go sensation is the *relaxation response*, which you want to get better at. Interestingly, relaxation is something that you cannot get better at by trying harder—like falling asleep or sexual arousal. You will get better at relaxing merely by focusing on what relaxation or "letting go" feels like. Memorize the sensations, and then simply try to reproduce the sensations.

Do this clenching exercise again and touch your right biceps muscle while you are clenching. You may notice some tension in your biceps that you were not aware of. One of the goals in practicing progressive muscle relaxation is to increase your awareness of where in your body your muscles are tense. If you don't know where your muscle tension resides, you can't do anything about it. You can't voluntarily reduce or lower tension if you don't know where it is.

Releasing Tension in Your Major Muscle Groups

Now we want you to practice tensing the major muscle groups in your body. One at a time, follow the instructions and tense up each of the muscle groups listed. Hold the tension in each muscle group for at least five to ten seconds, and then focus on relaxing and letting go for about ten seconds before going on to the next muscle group. As you practice these exercises, we want you to focus on what it feels like when you tense up and then what it feels like when you relax. This exercise works best while lying down or sitting in a comfortable chair.

- Clench both fists ... and relax, getting your arms into a comfortable position.

- Bend your elbows, bringing both your arms toward your body, and tense your biceps ... and relax your biceps.

- Straighten your arms in front of you, reaching across the room, and tense your triceps ... and then relax your arms.

- Raise your eyebrows and wrinkle up your forehead ... and now, stop tensing your forehead. Relax and smooth it out. (If you are having trouble doing this, look in mirror, raise up your eyebrows, and you will notice horizontal furrows of tension in your forehead.)

- Frown or scowl ... and smooth out your forehead once more.

- Close your eyes really tight. Feel the tension in, around, and behind your eyes ... and relax your eyes, keeping your eyes closed gently, comfortably.

- Grin broadly from ear to ear. Feel the tension in your cheeks, around the corners of your mouth ... and relax your cheeks.

- Push the tip of your tongue hard against the roof of your mouth and study the tension ... and relax.

- Purse your lips. Press your lips together ... and relax your lips.

- Clench your jaws and study the tension throughout your jaws ... and relax your jaws and let your lips part slightly. (If your jaws are completely relaxed, your lips will always be parted slightly. It requires clenching of your jaw muscles to keep your mouth completely shut.)

- Push your head back and feel the tension in your neck. Then roll your head to the left, and then roll your head to the right. Now straighten your head and bring your chin forward against your chest. Hold the tension . . . and now relax.

- Take a deep breath and hold your breath . . . and relax. Just breathe normally and easily.

- Shrug your shoulders up. Now bring your shoulders back so you feel the tension in your shoulders and upper back . . . and relax.

- Tense your stomach by pressing out . . . and relax your stomach.

- Tense your stomach by pulling in . . . and relax again.

- Arch your back, making the small of your back quite hollow, and feel the tension along your spine . . . and relax your lower back.

- With your legs straight, point your toes away from your face . . . and then relax your legs.

- With your legs straight, bring your toes up toward your face. Bring your toes right up . . . and then relax your legs.

How was that? Did you notice some tension in your body that you weren't aware of before you did this exercise? Where in your body do you typically experience muscle tension when you experience stress or get upset?

_____

_____

Where in your body are you experiencing the most tension right now?

_____

_____

The Anxiety or Tension Thermometer

You can take your anxiety or tension "temperature," using a scale called the anxiety or tension thermometer—where 0 is the calmest you have ever been (awake and alert, but so relaxed that it would be difficult to move a single muscle in your entire body) and 100 is the worst feeling you've ever had (terrified, horrified, or like a volcano ready to erupt). Your score is always between these two end points of 0 and 100.

What is your tension score right now on the tension thermometer—between 0 and 100? _____

Your learning to relax deeply will be facilitated by listening to a recording of the relaxation instructions. We have developed a recording of the relaxation exercises, which is available on a CD-ROM and can be ordered on our Web site (www.healingthetrauma.com).

When Should You Practice the Relaxation Exercises?

We suggest you do relaxation exercises twice a day. Bedtime is one time that works well; this won't eat into any waking time, and may help you fall asleep and sleep more deeply. A second good time is when you wake up in the morning. It will give your day a good start and there are no negative side effects. But choose the time of day that works best for you.

You may do some of the relaxation exercises during the day while riding the bus, driving the car, or at work. For example, Dr. Kubany often tenses and relaxes his stomach muscles during meetings if he feels tense. Many people use driving time as "worry time" because they have nothing to do but think. Make your goal to be more relaxed when you get to your destination than when you got into the car (or bus).

Will you be willing to do this relaxation exercise twice a day for the next month? Yes _____ No _____

If you said yes, that is great! It will be a good use of your time, promote your long-term best interests, give you more energy to do the things you have to do, make you less reactive to minor stressors, and improve your general mood.

A Technique to Prevent the Cumulative Effects of Stress

It is surprising how many people become upset about something and then remain stressed all day. A classic example is the way many formerly battered women suffering from PTSD react to distressing trauma-related dreams. The dreams may not only wake them up in a state of panic, but many women continue to ruminate about their dreams to the extent that it may ruin their entire day. A nightmare is also a good example of a stressful event happening that you cannot change or undo. It serves absolutely no purpose to continue to fret about something you cannot change or undo.

You do not have to stay at a high level of tension after stressful events are over. Let's say that something happens that brings you up to a tension score of 70 on the tension thermometer. You don't have to stay at 70 all day. You can bring yourself down 20 or 30 points in five to ten minutes. To accomplish this, we are going to teach you a technique for decreasing the tension in your muscles after you have been exposed to a stressful event. The technique for regulating your level of stress involves scanning your body to identify which muscles are affected by the stressor, overtensing the affected muscles at a peak as long as you can, and then letting go.

When something happens that is potentially stressful (you are late or caught in traffic; someone gets mad at you; you are reminded of the abuse), you can do a body scan to identify where in your body you are experiencing tension. A body scan involves attending to the major muscle groups in your body—one at a time—to identify which muscle (or muscles) became more tense when the stressful event occurred. You can then overtense the affected muscles, hold them at a peak for at least five to ten seconds, and then relax and focus on letting go. Repeat this tension-release cycle until you are back down to where you were before the stressful event occurred.

Tensing and Then Letting Go Exercise

Now practice this technique. But first, make another assessment of how tensed or relaxed you are right now, using the tension thermometer. What is your tension score right now? _____

1. Do a body scan. Where in your body do you notice the most tension?

   _____

2. Make sure you are in a comfortable position in an armchair or couch. Take a couple of long, slow deep breaths, and let yourself relax for five to ten seconds.

3. Take a deep breath and hold your breath for five to ten seconds. Then, breathe out and just breathe normally and easily for five to ten seconds.

4. Overtense the muscles in your body where you feel the most tension. (For many, the most tension is often in the face, whether you are initially aware of this or not.) Hold the tension for five to ten seconds, and then relax, focusing on letting go for ten to fifteen seconds.

5. Now take your tension temperature. What is your tension score right now? _____ Do you feel any better?

6. Repeat steps 3 and 4 if your tension score is still higher than 30.

In summary, it is very important that you tense and relax after experiencing stress. You do not have to stay stressed all day. If you are relaxed, you will not only feel better, you will also think more clearly.

Ways to Increase Body Awareness

Practicing the relaxation exercises and doing body scans when encountering stressful events should increase your body awareness and your awareness of which muscles tense up when you experience stress. However, we would like you to have increased body awareness throughout the day. One way of doing this is to get in the habit of scheduling body scans at regular times throughout the day—such as before or after meals, or at 8 A.M., noon, 4 P.M., and 8 P.M. If you have a digital watch with an hourly alarm feature, you might use it to do regular body scans. Such exercises might be particularly valuable if you tend to dissociate or space out a lot or are having difficulties increasing your body awareness.

What did you learn from this chapter?

_____

_____

_____

_____

CHAPTER 7

Why PTSD Persists and a
Path to Your Recovery

In this chapter, you will learn about a model of emotional learning that explains the development and persistence of PTSD in terms of psychological principles of learning. This model of learning was originally developed and demonstrated with animals, but the principles apply just as well to human learning as to animal learning. The model also suggests a way to treat PTSD, because if you have learned through conditioning to be afraid, you can also learn to overcome your fears.

Escape and Avoidance Learning and How It Works

First, we are going to describe and discuss how escape and avoidance learning occurs in animals. Then, we will explain how the same principles apply to escape and avoidance learning in people, and how these principles can account for the development and persistence of PTSD.

Look at the illustration on the next page. This enclosure is called a *shuttle box* and has a hurdle in the middle separating the two sides. And there is a laboratory mouse—whom we call "Millie." Millie can shuttle back and forth from one side of the box to the other. But when Millie is first placed in the box, she vastly prefers the left-hand side because this side is air-conditioned and there's plenty of food and water. The left side also has a light. Millie doesn't like the other side at all because it is always dark and humid, and Millie is only fed bland food and warm water once a day there.

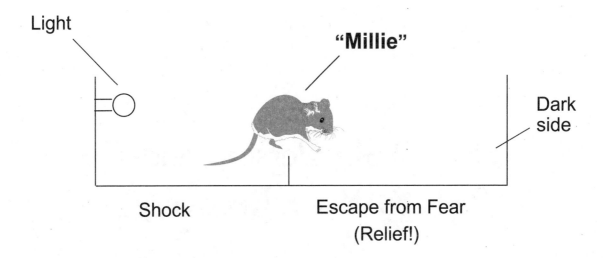

A Model of Emotional Learning and Escape and Avoidance Learning that Explains the Development and Persistence of PTSD

Unfortunately, the side with the light also has a floor with an electrified grid, which the mouse psychologist can turn on or off. Let's say the psychologist turns the light on and then gives Millie a shock. And let's say he does this again five or ten times.

What will Millie start thinking about the light? What will be her attitude about the light? Will she like it?

_____

_____

Millie will learn to dislike the light. This is *emotional learning*. If you repeatedly pair, connect, or associate something that is neutral (something that has no positive or negative associations) with something that has the power to evoke positive or negative feelings without prior learning—after a while the neutral event will also evoke positive or negative feelings. Millie leans to associate electric shock with light, so she avoids the light.

This kind of emotional learning was discovered by the Russian physiologist Ivan Pavlov, who taught a dog to like a musical tone. Pavlov experimented by turning on this tone just before showing a hungry dog a piece of meat. Hungry animals will instinctually salivate in the presence of food. When Pavlov repeatedly paired the onset of the tone with the presentation of the meat, the dog began to associate the tone with food. Eventually Pavlov turned on the tone but did not present the meat and the dog salivated. She learned to like the tone because the sound of the tone was repeatedly associated with something that she liked.

The same conditioning process works with people too, and can work to elicit a negative response. Let's say we put a picture on the wall of an extremely handsome man. And every time we illuminate this man's face, you get a shock in the seat of your chair. Would you like this guy? Of course not. And if we told you we wanted you to meet somebody, and this handsome man came into the room—and you could see the resemblance with the man in the picture—would you want to meet this guy? You would learn to avoid him.

After a while, what will Millie learn to do when the light goes on? She will jump to the other side. Millie gets a sense of relief from jumping to the other side.

The Power of Relief

Relief is a very, very powerful reward or reinforcer. A *reinforcer* is anything that someone likes, wants, and is willing to work for. In states of physical or emotional pain, people like, want, and are willing to work very hard to get relief! In states of pain, people will do almost anything to get relief. Relief is such a powerful reward that at least two antacid commercials have used the word *relief* in the slogan.

One of the problems with relief reinforcement is that it only feels good for a little while. For example, how many people would say that the best day of their life was the day they got over the stomach flu? It really felt great when they woke up, and their headache and nausea were gone. But, what about three days later? Are they still remembering how good it felt when they woke up three days ago? Relief only feels good when it is right next to pain—when it is immediately connected or associated with the termination of pain.

Another major problem with relief is that behaviors that lead to relief are usually not good for you. Relief-seeking behavior is the major reason that people come to psychotherapy. They are acting in ways to get immediate gratification or relief when the long-term consequences of their actions are self-defeating or self-destructive. Behaviors that lead to relief are not usually in your best interest, and behaviors that lead to relief or immediate gratification maintain or perpetuate all kinds of maladaptive behavior and psychopathology. Alcoholism and drug addiction are good examples of this. In the presence of withdrawal symptoms, a drug addict will do almost anything to get relief from the withdrawal symptoms—even if all the long-term consequences are negative—such as going to jail, getting more severely addicted, or engaging in behaviors that violate fundamental values, such as robbing or stealing, stealing from family, and even prostitution.

People addicted to drugs are the ultimate hedonists who will do anything to remove or terminate the pain of the withdrawal symptoms. "Boy, it feels so good when I put that needle in my arm." But, clearly it is not good for them in the long run to use drugs. Unfortunately, the negative side effects don't come until later. The relief happens right away—immediately, right now.

Obsessive-compulsive disorder is just one psychiatric problem that can be very well explained in terms of relief-seeking behavior. The psychologist says to his client, "Your hands look terrible. Red and raw. And they're infected. You must be washing your hands one hundred times a day! I bet it feels good when you wash your hands." "It does," says the client. For how long? Five minutes? And then she starts feeling anxious and "dirty" again so she washes her hands again to get temporary relief.

More than a few battered women are repeatedly badgered to engage in unwanted sex or unwanted sex acts—such as extremely long sex, anal sex, group sex, even prostitution—and give in to get relief from the badgering ("to get it over with . . . to get some peace . . . to get through the day . . . so I can get some sleep")—even though the long-term consequences of giving in are deep resentment, shame, and low self-esteem.

Now, let's go back to Millie and her relief-seeking behavior.

First, Millie learns to escape the light—to jump over the hurdle into the other compartment when the light goes on. After a while she also learns to avoid the light. Given a choice, Millie will stay on the other side and never go near the compartment with the light. Such escape and avoidance habits are very durable habits and hard to eliminate. Let's say the mouse psychologist starts feeling very sorry for Millie and throws the shock machine away. But he still keeps turning the light on once in a while. Millie will keep jumping to the other side—and she may never stop—even though she never gets shocked again.

Escape and avoidance habits are very durable for at least three reasons. Millie illustrates all three. First, each time Millie jumps over the hurdle she gets a big relief, which feels very good. A second reason Millie doesn't overcome her fear of the light is that she doesn't stay around long enough to find out that the light isn't dangerous. A third reason Millie doesn't overcome her fear and still wants to escape and avoid has to do with emotional reasoning. Let's assume that Millie has the power of language. Here's the scenario:

The light goes on. Millie notices her heart beating faster. She might say, "I don't feel safe. I wouldn't be afraid of the light if it weren't dangerous. My heart wouldn't be racing and I wouldn't be feeling unsafe. The light must be dangerous. I had better get out of here." Then, she jumps to the other side and notices her heart rate slowing down and says, "I feel safer now. I feel better when I get away from the light. That's additional proof it's safer over here and that the light must be dangerous."

When the light went on, Millie used her increase in symptoms and her thought that she felt unsafe as evidence that the light was dangerous. When she jumped to the other side, she interpreted her reduction in symptoms and her thought that she feels safer as evidence that the light had to be dangerous. Why else would she feel better and safer now? But is the light dangerous?

The shock machine is long gone, and Millie is actually safe now. Millie is being irrational and using her increase and decrease in anxiety as evidence. But Millie's anxiety symptoms are not evidence. The fact that Millie felt unsafe was not evidence that she was (or was not) in danger. The fact that she later felt safer was not evidence that she was then safe. Millie might think that she couldn't possibly be this scared if she weren't in real danger. But the intensity of her fear of the light is not evidence that she is in danger—just as the intensity of fear in a bad dream is not evidence that someone is in danger. This is emotional reasoning and has nothing to do with logic or fact.

What Do Millie and the Light Have to Do with PTSD?

Now, what does all this have to do with PTSD? Images, memories, and other reminders of traumatic events are just like the light. They are not dangerous. For example, imagining yourself getting hit in the stomach cannot cause physical pain,

Dr. Kubany was doing guided imagery with a woman afraid of swimming in deep water. He asked her to close her eyes and to visualize herself swimming in water over her head. When he told her to open her eyes, she said she had not conjured up the image. Dr. Kubany asked her to try again. After several seconds, the woman exclaimed, "I can't! I can't!" Dr. Kubany responded, "Imagining yourself swimming in deep water is not dangerous. Imagining yourself swimming in deep water cannot cause you to drown."

Any neutral—or even positive event—that is paired with or associated with a traumatic event will become disliked and avoided. Some rape victims who were raped in their showers will not take showers. Or if they do, they will take really short ones, because while they're in the shower they feel anxious, and when they get out of the shower, they get relief reinforcement. Some women who were raped in their own bed will no longer sleep in a bed. They would rather sleep on a couch, or if there is no couch, may actually prefer to sleep on the floor. One woman said, "I have to get over this." She got in bed, tossed and turned for half an hour, unable to sleep, and then got out of bed—thereby getting relief—and promptly fell asleep on her bumpy couch.

One of our clients had been raped in a studio apartment. She vowed never again to live in a studio apartment. Are studio apartments inherently dangerous? Of course not. You would be surprised how many women in our therapy for battered women program in Hawaii were assaulted by their husbands or boyfriends at the beach. Many of these women refuse to go to the beach anymore.

How Chronic Escape and Avoidance Behaviors Cause PTSD Symptoms to Persist

The major problem with this persistent escape and avoidance behavior—now that the trauma is over and the situation is no longer dangerous—is that it is maintaining or perpetuating PTSD. Escape and avoidance behaviors are relief-seeking behaviors that serve to maintain PTSD and depression. Millie's escape and avoidance behaviors are preventing her from overcoming her fear of the light. In similar ways, escape and avoidance behaviors have maintained your PTSD. It works something like this: You find yourself thinking about the abuse, and you get it out of your mind as quickly as possible. The relief that you get when you escape the thoughts is causing your symptoms to persist. Similarly, elaborate strategies to avoid being reminded of your abuse will keep you in a chronic state of relief—just like Millie was when she stayed on the dark, humid side of the enclosure. Relief-seeking behavior causes PTSD to persist just as relief-seeking behaviors cause addictions and obsessive-compulsive disorder to persist.

Unfortunately, many women who have been abused engage in chronic avoidance strategies. They often become more and more withdrawn, more and more isolated. They end up in states of chronic avoidance and relief, which no longer feels good at all, in an effort to get rid of every single reminder cue.

A Fear and Loss Model of PTSD

So far, we have been talking about a fear model of PTSD. But, in trauma, there are also important losses. Look at the case of a woman who was assaulted in her shower. She used to love taking showers. Now, if she takes a shower, it's a fast one. She feels anxious while taking the shower and gets out quickly so she can get relief. This woman's loss needs to be grieved, or her interest in taking showers needs to be rekindled in some way.

Many women who were assaulted on the beach by their husbands or boyfriends experience anxiety at the mere thought of going to the beach. But many of these women used to love the beach. That's where they may have met their boyfriends and had barbecues and beach parties. It's where they went with family and had the dream of growing old with their soul mate and dreams of the children always having their father in an intact family. These dreams have been shattered, and these losses need to be grieved.

Some losses are irreversible, and acceptance or peace of mind may only be achievable by grieving—which may be facilitated by weeping or sorrowful tears. For example, a marital betrayal and violent assault cannot be undone. Neither can permanent injuries or scars from the abuse; or a woman's experience of seeing her children witness domestic violence; or an unhappy childhood or years of physical or sexual abuse while growing up.

Other losses, however, are at least theoretically reversible: for example, losses in pleasure from activities you enjoyed before you were abused by your boyfriend or husband—especially activities you may have done together or that remind you of him—such as playing golf or tennis; watching certain programs on TV; eating certain foods; spending time with people whom you both knew; or going certain places, such as the beach or specific restaurants. You can do these things again.

What are some activities you used to enjoy that you may doubt you could ever enjoy again or doubt that you could enjoy again as much as you used to?

_____

_____

_____

In chapter 14, we will suggest some exercises that may help you rekindle your interest in these or other activities that you used to enjoy or avoid doing now.

Breaking Escape and Avoidance Habits and Recovery from PTSD

The reason this model of escape and avoidance learning is important is that it has implications for the treatment of PTSD. Millie's fear of the light is irrational. There is nothing to be afraid of. Not only that, the other side of the compartment is air-conditioned, there is plenty of food and water, there are even mouse magazines and a light to read by. Who knows, maybe there is even a mouse companion over there! These are all things Millie used to enjoy. And the shock—the trauma—is long gone. Yet, Millie prefers the side that is dark and humid, where she gets bland food once a day, and she does not want to go over to the side with the light. To do so makes her sad and anxious. If you put Millie on the side with the light, she will jump right over to the other side.

Okay, you have just been appointed to be Millie's psychologist. Millie is being extremely irrational. Your job now is to teach Millie to get over her irrational fear of the light. Remember, the light is just a light. It is not dangerous or capable of directly causing any pain. But somehow it has all this power. How are you going to teach Millie that the light isn't dangerous? Hint: You need to rearrange the enclosure so that the light is inescapable. Imagine that you're an architect or home decorator and can rearrange things anyway you want.

You could put up a wall on the side with the light so Millie can't get away from the light. Or you could put a light on both sides of the box so that no matter where Millie goes she will be exposed to the light.

How will Millie act at first when the light goes on? And what about after an hour?

_____

_____

_____

At first Millie will freak out. After an hour, if nothing else, Millie will be exhausted. And she might look up at the light and say, "Well, I'll be darned. It isn't dangerous." This is called *escape and avoidance busting*—exposing trauma survivors to harmless trauma reminders until the reminders lose their ability to evoke negative feelings.

All interventions shown to be effective for treating PTSD incorporate escape and avoidance busting as an important treatment component (Resick et al. 2002). All these interventions expose clients to "scary" reminders of the trauma that are just like the light—not actually harmful or dangerous. Avoidance busting is an important part of our program too. Escape and avoidance busting is one of the paths to recovery from PTSD.

A Circumstance under Which Prolonged Exposure Will Not Overcome Your Fear

There is one circumstance under which Millie could be repeatedly exposed to the light and not get over her fear. Do you have any idea what that circumstance might be? It's something like this: Millie is put in the compartment and the light goes on. And this is what she says: "Damn light. I never should have come into this box. I wasted five years of my life. How stupid. I could have prevented all this. And that mouse psychologist. What a monster. He promised he would be good to me. How could anyone be that cruel?"

These emotionally charged words are psychological shocks that recharge neutral memories and images of the abuse and the abuser with negative energy. What is happening is called *higher order language conditioning*. If you pair or associate negative words ("ugly . . . stupid . . . old . . . weak") with something neutral—for example, the color blue—the neutral something will become unliked. For example, you could teach your children to dislike the color blue by always talking about blue in negative terms. It is because negative words recharge your memories of abuse that one of our first orders of business—starting in chapter 4—was to help you change your language. If you stop using negative words when you think about the abuse and your abuser, you may still feel anxious and sad. But eventually the sadness and anxiety will dissipate and go away.

Exposing Yourself to Abuse- and Abuser-Related Reminders

In chapter 14, we are going to ask you to engage in several exercises to systematically expose yourself to reminders of your abuse and your abuser that are *not* harmful or dangerous. If you are courageous, you may want to start doing some of these exposure activities now. You might try activities you used to enjoy but now avoid doing because they remind you of your ex-partner.

What did you learn from reading this chapter and answering the questions posed?

_____

_____

_____

_____

CHAPTER 8

Overcoming the Attitude That You're Overwhelmed or Have No Power

Let's take a look at two different women confronting the same problem:

Woman #1: I'll never get over this wall. It's way too high. I tried getting over this wall before. It didn't work then, and it won't work now. I couldn't get over this wall when I came in here, and I can't get over this wall now. I could give you twenty reasons why I'm not going to get over this wall. I feel overwhelmed by this wall.

Woman #2: How can I get over this wall? How can I get through this wall? How can I get around this wall? How can I find a way to get to the other side? There must be some way.

Which of these two women do you think is most likely to be successful in getting to the other side of the wall?

In this chapter, you will learn how many battered women learn the obstacle-oriented, reasons-why-not thinking style expressed by woman number 1. You will also learn why many battered women continue to think this way even after they are safely out of an abusive relationship. To help you understand this thinking or cognitive style, we are going to teach you about a model of learned helplessness or learned powerlessness that has been widely used as a model of depression and "give-up-itis." This model is an expansion of what we talked about in chapter 7. We are also going to teach you about the importance of cultivating a solution-oriented or problem-solving thinking style, like that expressed by woman number 2, as a means of empowering you and facilitating your recovery from PTSD.

Learned Powerlessness

Imagine that Millie the mouse has been placed in a shuttle box like the one we described in the last chapter, but we want you to assume now that Millie has never been here before. This time there are no escape routes to the other side of the enclosure. In fact, Millie doesn't even know there is another side to the box.

The mouse psychologist turns on the light and then gives Millie a shock. Let's say he does this a hundred times today. And he turns the light on and shocks Millie a hundred times tomorrow, and the day after that too. What will Millie do at first when she is placed in the box and is shocked?

She will freak out. She will run frantically all over trying to find some way to escape or get away from the shock. And how will Millie behave after two or three days of getting shocked over and over again? For example, if you were looking at Millie, what do you think she would be doing?

_____

_____

The answer is, she wouldn't be doing anything. She would appear to have given up. And this is exactly what dogs did in the initial research on learned helplessness, which was conducted in the 1950s—before there were strict ethical standards for conducting research with animals (Seligman 1974). After prolonged exposure to inescapable shock, the dogs lay down and just moaned when the shock was turned on.

Millie will no longer try to get away from the shock. But has she really given up? Let us ask you this: Would it make sense for Millie to continue to try to get away if she can't escape—if escape is impossible?

_____

_____

It actually would not make any sense. For example, imagine that you are tied to a chair and someone is beating you with a stick. Would it make sense for you to focus on how much it hurts each time you get hit? Or would it make more sense for you to dissociate, daydream, or try to distract yourself in some way—to minimize the impact of the beating and the pain?

Of course it would. In addition, if you couldn't escape, would it make sense for you to use up the precious little energy you have left? Of course it wouldn't. So Millie hasn't really given up, has she? No, she hasn't. This is what she has done: she has shifted her focus from efforts to escape to efforts to survive—coping for survival.

Something very similar happens to many women who are in abusive relationships. Early on in the relationship, many battered women come to believe they are in the relationship permanently or cannot escape or get out of the relationship. Maybe they believe this because of ideas that marriage is supposed to be forever, or that they have to keep their marital vows, or that the children need their father. Maybe they believe threats by their partner that they will be harmed or killed if they try to leave. Others who have grown up with domestic violence may believe that all relationships are likely to be violent, and if they leave, the next relationship will be just as bad, maybe even worse.

Did you ever go through a period of time when you thought that you were going to be with your abuser forever—that there was no way that you would be able to get out of the relationship? Yes _____ No _____ If yes, what were your reasons for believing that you would not be able to end the relationship or leave your partner?

_____

_____

What Do Battered Women Do?

Women are very creative and keep trying to come up with new ways to stop the abuse. After all, their partner repeatedly blamed them for the abuse and would ask, "Why do you keep making me hit you?"

Asked what new ways she came up with to stop the abuse, one client said, "I stopped having an opinion. I stopped bringing up things that bothered me or issues that mattered to me because it would only infuriate and enrage him. If I noticed he was in a bad mood, I would avoid him. Another way to avoid it was to participate in his drinking or smoking. So I did things that went against my upbringing. In essence, I lost myself to try to avoid it. And it got worse. Worse and worse."

What are some of the ways you came up with to try to get your partner to stop abusing you?

_____

_____

Eventually, women learn that there is nothing they can do to stop the abuse. More than one woman has said, "I could do absolutely nothing, and he would still beat me up." Research by Neil Jacobson and colleagues (Jacobson et al. 1994) confirms that battered women do not have the power to stop the abuse. They studied communication styles in couples with a violent husband. The abusive husbands acknowledged that once violence begins there is nothing the wife can do to stop it. Even strategies such as withdrawal do not suppress the violence or its escalation.

One of our clients was in a relationship with an abusive man who came and went as he pleased. He came home one day after being gone for several days, and she was terrified about what he might do. She said absolutely nothing and went into her bedroom and sat on the bed. He came into the bedroom, watched her for a half hour—without saying anything—and then he beat her up.

Marie's Story

We will give you an extreme example of a woman who believed that she was trapped in an abusive relationship and believed she was completely powerless to prevent even the worst possible outcome. Marie was using numbness and dissociation to cope with what she perceived as a completely hopeless situation. One day, her boyfriend said, "I am going to kill you today." They were driving to the north shore of Oahu. Marie's boyfriend stopped to go into a 7-Eleven convenience store to buy some beer and left Marie in the car. She did not even try to get away. She just sat in the car and stared off into space. As it turned out, Marie wasn't killed, or we wouldn't be able to tell you this story. However, the story illustrates how women who feel trapped in abusive relationships do not engage in problem-solving coping and instead use emotion-focused coping to minimize the impact of painful situations perceived to be unsolvable.

Once they learn that they are powerless to stop the abuse, many women start numbing out and focusing on the bread crumbs of good things about the relationship—to make the best of a bad situation. For example: "He isn't always mean. He really is a nice guy."

One client said, "I would inflate every little thing. Everyone at work thought he was so great. His cooking. He's very religious. He really does have a good heart. All the good things about him. I would puff up everything in my mind."

What are some of the positive little things that you focused on to make the best out of a bad situation?

_____

_____

Other people can't understand why a battered woman focuses on the positive. But if a woman believes she can't get out of an abusive relationship and is powerless to stop the abuse, it would be pointless to focus on the abuse. It makes more sense to dissociate and focus on something else.

There have been stories of people who were lost in the Arctic who survived for weeks without food or water. They survived by focusing on preserving precious resources—with very low body temperatures and moving as little as possible. These efforts to cope were clearly not efforts to escape; they were efforts to survive.

What Happens When the Psychologist Takes the Wall Down?

Let's say the mouse psychologist starts feeling sorry for Millie and takes down the wall so that escape is possible. Millie sees the other side and says, "Wow, I didn't know there was another side to this box." Now, what will Millie do when the light goes on and then the shock goes on? Will she stay where she is or will she jump to the other side?

Millie stays where she is. Millie doesn't jump because she doesn't think it would do any good. All her prior efforts to escape were futile, so she has acquired the pervasive belief that she has no power—that she is incapable of stopping bad things from happening through efforts of her own. Therefore, it would be pointless to focus on the pain and to try and get away.

Learned powerlessness training has been conducted with elephants to make the elephants more compliant. Trainers chain the elephant's leg to a cage or some other immovable object, and each time the elephant tries to get away, the chain hurts the elephant's leg. Eventually, the elephant stops trying to get away because trying to get away not only doesn't do any good, it causes pain. Can you now understand why elephants who are tied to a rope and peg in the ground do not try to get away—even though they have the power to easily get away? Perceived reality is more important than actual reality.

The kind of learned powerlessness training used with the elephant is probably more efficient and effective than the learned powerlessness training with dogs described earlier, because efforts to escape are not only futile, but they result in an increase or escalation of pain. Relate this to the situation of many battered women, whose efforts to stop the abuse or to escape from the relationship not only don't work, they result in an escalation of the abuse or other negative consequences.

In laboratory studies, humans have been taught to believe they are helpless. For example, human subjects have been taught to endure and not try to escape mild shock—even though they have the potential power to escape the shock (Rosenhan and Seligman 1989). Subjects were asked to put their finger on a table, and when they did, they received a mild electrical shock. When they picked up their finger, which was the reflexive thing to do, they continued to receive the shock. After a while, the experimenter arranged it so that if subjects raised their finger the shock would go off. However, subjects who had learned that raising their finger didn't do any good continued to keep their finger on the table and continued to receive the shock—even though the shock was now escapable.

Learning How to Overcome Learned Helplessness

Because Millie doesn't try to get away from the shock, she has no opportunities to learn that going to the other side will terminate the pain. To encourage Millie, let's say we coax her to the other side where she gets relief from the shock. "Wow, that feels great," says Millie. Now we put her back on the side with the light and turn on the light and the shock—what will Millie do?

_____

Many of our clients say that now Millie will jump to the other side. And when they do, we say, "We would like to think that Millie will jump, but she doesn't. Why not?" Why do you think Millie will not jump to the other side even after she has had the experience of relief when she gets to the other side?

_____

_____

Let's interview Millie to find out why she didn't try to get away from the light.

_Us:_   Millie, didn't you notice that the shock went off when we coaxed you to the other side?

Millie: Yeah. That was great!

_Us:_   Well, then why didn't you go to the other side when the light went on?

Millie: What would be the point?

_Us:_   What do you mean, "What would be the point?" Didn't you notice that you got relief when you got to the other side?

Millie: Yeah, I noticed. That was great!

_Us:_   Well, why do you think the shock went off?

Millie: I don't know, but it didn't have anything to do with me. Was he having a good day? Did he find some other mouse to pick on?

The point here is that Millie has acquired the pervasive belief that she is powerless—that she cannot stop bad things from happening. She sees no relationship or connection between her behavior and good and bad things that happen to her.

The bad news here is that Millie is a slow learner. The good news is that she eventually does learn to get away from the shock. Animals who have been taught to be powerless are slow to learn to get away from the shock when it is no longer inescapable—even if you coax them to the other side of the compartment, and they experience the shock going off. Left to themselves on the side with the shock, they may remain curled up on the floor and endure the shock. Eventually, however, the animals will learn to escape and avoid the shock. That's the good news.

Now, what does all this have to do with formerly battered women? Something very similar happens to many battered women after they are safely out of an abusive relationship. They still do not feel very powerful. Many women who are now safely out of abusive relationships still believe they are very uninfluential and are not good at getting their way with other people. They may think that if they get involved in a new relationship, they still won't be able to get their needs met and will be taken advantageous of—or worse. Let us give you a few examples.

Mary's Story

Mary had a very good marriage for about ten years. Then something really bad happened to one of her husband's close friends, and this activated memories of some terrible trauma from his childhood. Overnight, he turned from a nice guy to a "screamer." He would repeatedly scream at Mary, six inches away from her face. Mary believed he was sick and that she had to see him through his illness. So she would just take it and would dissociate or shut down to minimize the impact of the screaming. Mary shut down so much, in fact, that she could only remember about one month out of a two-year period of time.

If her husband wasn't home by 9 P.M., Mary knew that he was drinking and that she would be in for it when he got home. On these occasions, she would go into the closet, crawl under a pile of clothes, and roll up into a ball—as if to try to shrink and disappear. When she came to therapy, she was divorced, safe, and had a good job. She was under a lot of stress, however, and her PTSD symptoms were acting up. One day Mary misplaced her keys three times and was being very self-critical—"What's the matter with me? Why can't I get over this?"—which did not help matters. To make matters worse, her coworker (who was a very nice guy) started making fun of her ("How can anyone misplace their keys three times in one day in a small office like this?"). Mary did not think he was being funny, however, and referred to his behavior as "picking on me." She said, "Why do people always pick on me?" Well, her coworker drove Mary home after work as he often did and went with her into her apartment to have a cup of coffee as he often did. When Mary walked into her apartment, she walked through the living room, went into her bedroom, closed the door, and rolled up into a ball! She acted as if she was just as powerless and out of control as she truly was when she was trapped in her marriage. It never even occurred to Mary to say something like, "Hey, get off my case," or "Can you at least help me look for my keys?" or "I don't think your teasing is funny and would appreciate your stopping!"

There is a related story about Mary that further illustrates just how powerless or uninfluential she believed herself to be. Mary described other coworkers in her office as extremely malicious and exploitative. For example, she said, "They really have it in for me." Mary's therapist started talking to her about the importance of being assertive and standing up for her rights. Her therapist said, "People can't read your mind and will not know what you want or what bothers you if you don't tell them" and encouraged Mary to start advocating for herself. Mary's first reaction to this suggestion was to recoil in fear. She said that if she started being assertive, it not only would not help, it would make matters worse. "Then, they will *really* have it in it for me," said Mary. Can you see just how powerless she perceived herself to be?

Yuriko's Story

A second example of a formerly battered woman who continued to believe that she was not in control of her life—even though she had been out of an abusive relationship for three years—is Yuriko. Yuriko was dreading having to move, and we couldn't figure out why. Yuriko came to a therapy session reporting great shame for something she had done. A friend who was going to help her move called at the last minute and said she couldn't help because she just got a job. Yuriko said that she felt overwhelmed when her friend told her she couldn't help, and she ended up taking some illegal drugs to deal with her feelings. And now she felt like a bad mother to her two young boys. Yuriko's therapist asked her to try and remember the first time she "felt overwhelmed." Almost instantly, Yuriko said that she first felt this way when she was five years old, living with an abusive stepmother. Yuriko said that on this occasion, her stepmother was going out and told her "to do this, and this, and this, and this"—giving Yuriko a series of impossible tasks. Yuriko knew she would be beaten when her stepmother returned home, no matter how much she did. Was Yuriko overwhelmed in this situation? She certainly was. She had absolutely no power and could not do anything to prevent the bad things that were going to happen to her. Now Yuriko felt just as overwhelmed having to move as she did when given impossible tasks by her stepmother. Yuriko's therapist asked her, "How is having to move as an adult similar to being given an overwhelming task as a small child?" Yuriko answered, "They aren't the same at all. Except I felt the same way!"

Yuriko was using emotional reasoning to conclude that she was just as powerless as an adult as she was when she was a small child. As her present situation was analyzed, Yuriko realized that she was not overwhelmed and did in fact have many options. She now realized that what she really needed to do—instead of taking drugs—was to relax and prioritize the tasks involved in moving.

Lucille's Story

A client named Lucille had a history of extremely brutal partner abuse and regularly used emotional numbing and dissociation as her primary ways of coping—to get relief from the memory of chronic abuse that went on for years. Lucille was now safely out of the abusive relationship and had recently moved to Hawaii. A friend was helping her learn the bus routes, and they were a mile from their car. They started walking back to the car, but an old leg injury started acting up. Lucille said she needed to rest and asked her friend get the car and then come back to pick her up. Lucille was waiting for her friend to come back in a secluded park, when a small group of men and women—who were obviously high on drugs—came up to her and tried to entice her to take some drugs. Lucille was terrified. Lucille laid down on the grass, put her head down, and closed her eyes. Clearly, this was not problem-solving coping.

Solution-Oriented Thinking

A learned helplessness outlook or attitude focuses on obstacles and reasons why problems cannot be solved. What are your chances of getting over a high wall if you focus or dwell on how high it is, citing reasons why you can't get over it?

The answer is slim to none, not good at all. You're only going to get over that wall if you get lucky—and that wouldn't have anything to do with you or anything you have control over.

One client was asked her chances of getting over a wall if she didn't think she could get over it, and she said, "I wouldn't even think about the wall!" This is a classic example of learned powerlessness thinking, where the empahsis is on emotion-focused coping—adaptive if you can't escape from a bad situation, but maladaptive if escape routes exist.

We define *coping* as acting to minimize the impact of adverse or painful events. There are two very different ways of minimizing the impact of physically or emotionally painful events. *Emotion-focused coping* involves placing your focus on finding ways to get immediate relief from the impact of negative events—without doing anything to remove the aversive stimulus or solve the underlying problem. You may be using emotion-focused coping to find ways to feel better about a physically or emotionally painful situation, which you may perceive as unsolvable. Examples of emotion-focused coping include

- avoiding memories of traumatic events

- emotional numbing

- dissociation

- use of alcohol or drugs

- overeating or bingeing and purging

- self-mutilation

Problem-solving coping involves efforts to solve a problem or to eliminate the source of discomfort. It involves placing your focus on overcoming difficulties, eradicating problems, finding solutions, or otherwise eliminating some irritant or aversive stimulus. This latter form of coping is what we advocate in this book.

We use problem solving to cope all the time, which is a reason we do not get depressed working with battered women and other trauma survivors. Can you imagine how depressing this kind of work would be if we focused on how bad our clients' problems are? We might think, "Oh my god, you're never going to be able to recover from this. You might as well give up and drop out of therapy right now. You're wasting your time. And I'm wasting my time too! I've got a headache. I need a drink. I need to get out of this line of work."

Wouldn't this be a terrible job if this was our attitude?

This solution-oriented or problem-solving attitude is the same kind of attitude that a former prisoner of war used to survive imprisonment. This POW never gave up hope, and never stopped trying to come up with ways to escape. Developing a solution-oriented attitude is going to facilitate and promote your recovery from PTSD, and it is necessary for your recovery. Coming up with ideas for possible solutions is incompatible with "give-up-itis" and perceptions of powerlessness.

Does this make sense? Can you relate to this? Can you see how an outlook that is always looking for solutions is going to be helpful or useful for you?

_____

_____

In the next chapter, we will look closely at the issue of guilt, an issue which many formerly battered women have and believe they are powerless to overcome. Then, in chapter 10, we will use cognitive trauma therapy to rid you of your guilt (if this is an issue for you) and to illustrate how solution-oriented thinking can work for you.

What did you learn from reading this chapter and answering the questions posed?

_____

_____

_____

_____

CHAPTER 9

Everything You Ever Wanted to Know about Guilt but Were Afraid to Ask

There is some good news and some bad news about guilt. First the bad news. Guilt is an extremely common source of pain and torment among trauma survivors. We will give you a few examples. Among 168 women in support groups for battered women, only 6 indicated they had no guilt related to the abuse (Kubany et al. 1996). Half of the 162 remaining women reported moderate or greater abuse-related guilt, and almost one in four reported considerable or greater guilt related to their victimization. In a study of 251 women with histories of physical and/or sexual abuse (for which most had recently sought treatment), 201 received a formal diagnosis of PTSD (Kubany 2000). Among the women who had PTSD, 75 percent had moderate or greater guilt related to their victimization, and almost 40 percent had considerable or greater guilt. Among 45 Vietnam veterans who had sought counseling for the effects of war stress in the past year, 82 percent reported moderate or greater combat-related guilt, and half (51 percent) reported guilt in the considerable to extreme range (Kubany et al. 1996).

Now the good news. Trauma survivors tend to exaggerate or distort the importance of their role in trauma. Survivors often experience guilt that has absolutely no rational or logical basis. They have been beating themselves up for nothing. Additional good news is that relief from your guilt is achievable. In our treatment-outcome studies of cognitive trauma therapy, we have helped more than 100 women get rid of most of their guilt. We are going to try to help you get rid of your guilt too.

Trauma, Guilt, and PTSD

In a study of fifty women receiving treatment for the effects of childhood sexual abuse, forty-three of the women (86 percent) strongly agreed with the following statement: "I was responsible for the abuse because it went on for so long (Jehu 1989)." These women accepted responsibility for their own victimization in spite of the fact that almost all of these women were first abused before the age of ten, and almost half were first abused before the age of six. Does this make any sense? While most of our clients agree that these beliefs are irrational, some clients also say, "I can understand how these women feel." We are going to tell you a few stories of trauma survivors whose faulty thinking led them to experience guilt that had no rational basis.

Joan's Story

Joan was the assistant manager of a bank and in charge on the day a man held up her bank. Pointing a gun at her, the robber took Joan hostage. He said that he had a bomb and threatened to kill everyone in the bank. Joan was traumatized by the robbery. When Joan called to make an appointment to receive therapy, she sobbed uncontrollably, saying that, "The reason I feel so bad is that a man died." Who do you think died? It was the robber. He was killed by the police as he opened the door just a crack. Joan "felt" that she was 90 percent responsible for the robber's death because she tiptoed toward the door with him by her side as he held a gun to her head. She was trying to get him away from the tellers and customers so they would be safer.

Sylvia's Story

Sylvia went to the circus and witnessed a raging elephant trample the trainer and turn toward the crowd before charging out of the auditorium. Sylvia experienced extremely severe guilt for not going down to the floor of the circus and giving mouth-to-mouth resuscitation to the trainer. She reasoned that she was obligated to do this because she had been trained in CPR, and her job involved health promotion. Sylvia was at the circus with her aunt, her sister, and her seven-year-old son, *and* she was pregnant.

Sylvia had multiple prior experiences of traumatization, including physical and sexual abuse by her stepfather. If anything went wrong at home, Sylvia was always blamed, and she always felt responsible. As a result of these experiences, Sylvia always took on a lot of guilt.

David's Story

David worked as an army medic in a remote jungle area in Vietnam during the Vietnam War. He was assigned to a small unit of twenty-five men whose mission was to set ambushes for the enemy. Five men at a time went out to set ambushes while the rest of the unit stayed at the base camp. On one occasion, the five men in the field accidentally walked into an underground enemy base camp and were ambushed. They called the base camp for assistance, and when the rest of the unit came to assist, they were ambushed too. In the firefight that ensued, David was attending to three wounded men at one time. He waved to a buddy for help. As the man approached to assist, he walked directly into the line of fire and was killed.

David was the first client with whom Dr. Kubany used a questionnaire called the Attitudes about Guilt Scale (AAGS) for helping to assess and analyze guilt. The AAGS assesses the magnitude of four guilt-related beliefs and the magnitude of distress and guilt related to specified guilt issues.

We asked him:

1. To what extent do you think that you should have known better and could have prevented or avoided the outcome?

2. How justified was what you did? (How good were your reasons for what you did?)

3. How personally responsible were you for causing what happened?

4. Did you do something wrong? (Did you violate personal standards of right and wrong by what you did?)

David endorsed each of these four guilt-related beliefs to the maximum degree. His answer to the first item was, "I absolutely should have known better." His answer to the second item was, "What I did (waving for help) was not justified in any way." His answer to the third item was, "I was completely responsible" (for the death of his friend). And his answer to the fourth item was, "What I did was extremely wrong." David also indicated that he always experienced extreme distress about the death of his friend and always experienced extreme guilt.

Now, was David being rational? Of course not. Completely irrational. For example, David didn't even give the enemy any credit or responsibility for the death of his friend.

Let's say we were conducting a group therapy session with Joan, Sylvia, David, and you. If we were going around and having everyone tell their story, you would probably be telling these people, "Lighten up. You're being too hard on yourself." Right? And then we would get around to you. You would probably say something like, "Well, my story is different because I deserve to feel guilty." We know that you probably do not agree now, but we are going to help you understand that your guilt is probably just as irrationally based as the guilt of the trauma survivors we just told you about.

The Nature of Guilt

Guilt can be defined as an unpleasant feeling with an accompanying belief that one should have thought, felt, or acted differently. Guilt is two things. Guilt involves bad or unpleasant feelings; but it also involves a set of beliefs, cognitions, interpretations, or negative value judgments about yourself. Because guilt has both a thinking part and a feeling part, we could just as appropriately say "I think guilty" as "I feel guilty"; however, it would probably be most technically correct to say "I experience guilt"—because this takes into account the fact that guilt has both a feeling part and a thinking part.

In our therapy for alleviating guilt (Kubany and Manke 1995), we take guilt apart and look at each part or component separately so that guilt is easier to understand. We analyze guilt issues by dealing with one issue at a time and by analyzing each part of guilt, one part at a time.

Looking at Four Guilt-Related Beliefs

Four guilt-related beliefs are assessed on the AAGS questionnaire, which you'll find at the end of this chapter. Question 1 assesses beliefs about foreseeability and preventability—"To what extent do you think you should you have known better and could have prevented or avoided the outcome?"—with five choices, from "There is no possible way that I could have known better" to "I absolutely should have known better."

The second question on the AAGS assesses beliefs about justification—soundness of reasons for actions taken: "How justified was what you did?"—with five choices, from "What I did was completely justified" to "What I did was not justified in any way."

A third guilt-related belief is assessed by question 3 on the AAGS—"How personally responsible were you for causing what happened?"—with five choices, from "I was in no way responsible for causing what happened" to "I was completely responsible for causing what happened." To the extent that you think you caused a negative outcome, you will experience guilt.

With responsibility, you can easily see that it is not just the presence or absence of these beliefs that is important. What is important is the magnitude of the beliefs. For example, if you feel only slightly responsible for causing a negative outcome, you will experience less guilt than if you think you are completely responsible for causing the outcome. By looking at guilt this way, you can also see why trauma-related guilt is usually much more severe than everyday guilt—such as guilt about hurting someone's feelings or forgetting an appointment (Kubany and Watson 2003). In trauma-related guilt, distress is often profound or severe, and distress is one of the components of guilt. When distress is severe, you only have to implicate yourself to slight degree to experience severe guilt.

The fourth question on the AAGS assesses wrongdoing—"Did you do something wrong? (Did you violate personal standards of right and wrong by what you did?)"—with five choices, from "What I did was not wrong in any way" to "What I did was extremely wrong." This is what people usually mean when they typically talk about guilt—religious guilt, sinning, violations of moral values.

Finally, the fifth question on the AAGS assesses the magnitude of your distress when you think about what happened—from no distress at all to extreme distress.

Published research has shown that knowing how a person answers the first five items on the AAGS can be used to accurately predict how much guilt the person will report (Kubany et al. 1995a). In other words, how guilty you feel about any guilt issue of yours can be estimated relatively accurately on the basis of

1. the degree to which you think you should have known better and could have prevented or avoided some negative outcome

2. how justified you think you were for acting as you did

3. how responsible you think you were for causing the negative outcome

4. the degree to which you think you violated values of right and wrong by what you did

5. how distressed you become when you think about what happened

Analyzing Guilt: Exercises in Logic

In our guilt therapy, we engage clients in several intellectual exercises in logic to help them think more clearly about their role in trauma. We address one guilt issue at a time, and one guilt component at a time. Our goal is to help our clients reach an accurate, objective, and realistic appraisal of their roles. We do not to try to fool our clients into believing something that isn't true.

In the next chapter, we will use the AAGS to engage you in our intellectual analysis of guilt in an attempt to help you get rid of some of your guilt. If you are a formerly battered woman with PTSD, you probably experience guilt about not leaving sooner—or any one of its variants, such as guilt about ever dating the abuser, moving in with him, marrying him, going back to him. Guilt about not having left sooner is far and away the most common guilt issue among formerly battered women with PTSD. If guilt about not having left sooner is not an issue for you, you will have an opportunity to see how analysis of this issue (and guilt issues in general) typically proceeds. We will also analyze another guilt issue that you identify for us, and we will try to help you to feel less guilty about this issue.

Note: Do not complete the AAGS now. We will ask you to complete it in chapter 10.

What did you learn from this chapter?

_____

_____

_____

_____

Attitudes about Guilt Survey (AAGS)

Individuals who have experienced traumatic events often experience guilt that is related to these events. They may feel guilty about something they did (or did not do), about beliefs or thoughts that they had (that they now believe to be untrue), or about having had certain feelings (or lack of feelings). The purpose of this questionnaire is to evaluate how you feel about one (and only one) guilt issue.

Please take a moment to think about your experience. Briefly describe what happened:

_____

_____

I should have / shouldn't have (circle one):_____

In answering each of the following questions, please circle one letter that best reflects or summarizes your view of what happened.

1. To what extent do you think that you should have known better and could have prevented or avoided the outcome?

    a. There is no possible way that I could have known better.

    b. I believe slightly that I should have known better.

    c. I believe moderately that I should have known better.

    d. For the most part I believe that I should have known better.

    e. I absolutely should have known better.

2. How justified was what you did? (How good were your reasons for what you did?)

    a. What I did was completely justified (excellent reasons).

    b. What I did was mostly justified.

    c. What I did was moderately justified.

    d. What I did was slightly justified.

    e. What I did was not justified in any way (very poor reasons).

3. How personally responsible were you for causing what happened?

    a. I was in no way responsible for causing what happened.

    b. I was slightly responsible for causing what happened.

    c. I was moderately responsible for causing what happened.

    d. I was largely responsible for causing what happened.

    e. I was completely responsible for causing what happened.

    Your percentage of responsibility? ____ percent

4. Did you do something wrong? (Did you violate personal standards of right and wrong by what you did?)

a. What I did was not wrong in any way.

b. What I did was slightly wrong.

c. What I did was moderately wrong.

d. What I did was very wrong.

e. What I did was extremely wrong.

5. How distressed do you feel when you think about what happened?

a. I feel no distress when I think about what happened.

b. I feel slightly distressed when I think about what happened.

c. I feel moderately distressed when I think about what happened.

d. I feel very distressed when I think about what happened.

e. I feel extremely distressed when I think about what happened.

6. Circle the answer that indicates how often you experience guilt that relates to what happened.

never   seldom   occasionally   often   always   whenever I think about it

7. Circle the answer which indicates the intensity or severity of guilt that you typically experience about what happened.

none   slight   moderate   considerable   extreme

CHAPTER 10

How to Get Rid of Your Guilt

In this chapter, you are going to learn about several thinking errors that lead trauma survivors to draw faulty guilt-related conclusions about their role in traumatic events. And we are going to try to help you get rid of some of your guilt.

Many battered women face a myriad of bad choices, which is one of many reasons why abuse-related guilt is extremely common among battered women. Faced with choices whereby they are damned if they do and damned if they don't, many battered women will experience guilt no matter what course of action they choose. Some battered women experience guilt for calling the police and "betraying" their partner, while others have guilt about not calling the police. Some battered women experience guilt about pressing charges, while others have guilt about not pressing charges (or recanting charges). Some battered women experience guilt about staying with the batterer, while others, who have left, experience guilt about depriving the children of their father. Some battered women experience guilt about reconciling with the batterer after having left, while others, who are staying away, feel sorry for the batterer.

Good News and Bad News

So again, the bad news is that many women with partner abuse–related PTSD have several abuse-related guilt issues. The good news is that in cognitive trauma therapy we have helped clients get rid of most of their guilt by analyzing only two or three of their guilt issues. The same thinking errors that contribute to faulty conclusions related to one guilt issue also contribute to faulty conclusions related to other guilt issues, so correcting your thinking errors on one guilt issue may enable you to autocorrect the same thinking errors on your other guilt issues.

Analyzing Guilt about Not Having Left Sooner

The most common guilt issue among formerly battered women is guilt about not having ended an abusive relationship sooner. The great majority of women we have treated in cognitive trauma therapy felt guilty about not having left sooner, and we have analyzed this issue with well over one hundred women. There are probably tens of thousands of American women who are plagued by this issue and its variations—such as guilt about reconciling with an abusive partner or guilt about marrying someone who was abusive or became abusive. This guilt is often linked to guilt about problems the children are having related to having witnessed domestic violence, because many women believe that if they had left sooner the children wouldn't be having these problems. When we resolve a woman's guilt about not having left sooner, guilt about problems the children are having usually dissolves as well.

If you are a formerly battered woman with partner abuse–related PTSD, chances are very good that guilt about not leaving sooner is an issue for you. In this chapter, we will analyze this issue to help you to get rid of it. Even if this is not an issue for you, read the next few pages to see how analyzing a guilt issue can be helpful. The method we will use applies to other guilt issues as well.

Completing the Attitudes about Guilt Survey (AAGS)

In cognitive trauma therapy, we begin our guilt intervention by having clients complete the AAGS (see chapter 9) with respect to the guilt issue selected for analysis and then we analyze each of the answers. If guilt about not leaving an abusive relationship sooner is an issue for you, we would like you to complete the AAGS as this issue relates to you. First, make two or three copies of the blank AAGS from chapter 9 so you can use it again for other guilt issues you may wish to analyze. After you have made copies, complete an AAGS with respect to guilt about not having left sooner.

At the top of the AAGS, briefly describe what happened and what you think you should have done differently. For example:

- "I should have left (name) sooner."

- "I shouldn't have moved in with (name)."

- "I shouldn't have married (name)."

- "I shouldn't have gone out with (name)."

- "I shouldn't have gone back to (name) after I left him."

When you get to question number 3 (the responsibility question), we would like you to answer this item twice, in two slightly different ways. The first time you answer it, we want to know how responsible you believe you were for staying with your abusive partner (on that day or point in time when you think you should have left). The second time you answer it, we want to know how responsible you think you are for the negative consequences associated with staying, such as continued abuse, problems the children developed because of exposure to violence, lowering of your self-esteem, loss of friends, or guilt and shame you are experiencing now for not having left sooner.

Reviewing What Happened Leading Up to the Day You "Should Have Left"

After clients complete the AAGS in cognitive trauma therapy, we ask them to give us a highly detailed, slow-motion description of what happened, leading up to the point in time that they think they should have left their abusive partner. We ask them to tell us exactly what happened, leading up to the specific day, situation, incident, or point in time when they think they should have left their abusive partner. If not leaving sooner is a guilt issue for you, when should you have left (or broken off the relationship)? Be very specific as to when.

_____

_____

_____

_____

The answers our clients give to this question vary. Sometimes clients say things like, "I should have moved out the first time he hit me." Or they may say, "I never should have married him." Other women say they should have left before they got pregnant or when their partner became overcontrolling, possessive, or jealous.

Analyzing Guilt—Part 1: Determining the Foreseeability and Preventability of the Negative Consequences of Staying

From here on, we are going to assume that not leaving sooner is a guilt issue for you, and we will help you analyze this issue. If not leaving sooner is not an issue for you, do not answer the questions we pose. However, read on and you will learn how our guilt analysis works with women who do have this issue.

Determining When You First Realized You Should Have Left

1. What should you have known better?

_____

_____

_____

We typically get answers like: "I should have known he wasn't going to change or that I wouldn't be able to change him . . . I should have known he was going to do it again . . . I should have known it was going to continue and get worse . . . I should have known he had the potential for violence before I married him . . . I should have known to leave before I got pregnant . . . I should have known from his reputation that I shouldn't have married him . . . I should have known how the children would be affected."

2. What are some of the negative outcomes you could have prevented if you had left when you think you should have left? Before you answer this question, we will tell you how some of our clients have answered this question: "I could have prevented years of abuse and humiliation . . . I could have prevented the guilt and shame I have for not having left sooner . . . I could have prevented the children from being exposed to domestic violence . . . I could have prevented the problems the kids are having right now . . . I could have prevented my overuse of alcohol or drugs to cope with the continuing abuse . . . I could have prevented losing my self-esteem . . . I could have prevented wasting some of the best years of my life . . . I could have prevented my isolation from friends and family . . . I could have prevented losing the opportunity to go back to school (or advance professionally) . . . I could have prevented being stuck in a low-paying job."

Now, we will ask you again. What are some of the negative outcomes that you could have prevented by leaving when you think you should have left?

_____

_____

3. What should you have done differently? Describe exactly what you think you should you have done and when you should have done this.

_____

_____

4. When did you first realize or learn that this was what you were supposed to do?

_____

In the great majority of cases, clients indicate they first realized or learned that this was what they were supposed to do after—oftentimes long after—the day or incident they specified as when they should have left.

From here on, we are going to assume that you now realize that you first learned with certainty that you should have left your abusive partner *after* you indicated you should have left (in item 1). Every once in a while, a client will insist that they did know in advance that they should have left sooner. If you still believe you knew in advance that you should have left but stayed instead, please bear with us. Later in this chapter, we will ask you additional questions about how you knew, and perhaps you will learn that you didn't know as much as you think you knew. In other words, perhaps some of the negative outcomes that you think were foreseeable—and therefore preventable—may not have been as foreseeable as you think they were.

Information You Acquire after Making a Decision Cannot Help You Make That Decision

Okay. You didn't realize you should have left until after the incident when you said you should have left. This is something like a woman saying she should have left the first time her husband hit her even though it never occurred to her that she should have left then until she went to a workshop on domestic violence two years later. The point is, you cannot use knowledge that you acquire or obtain after making a decision to guide or assist you in making the earlier decision. You cannot use information that you acquire on Wednesday to help you make a decision you made two days earlier, on Monday. You can't use knowledge that the stock market went up 500 points today to help you with an investment decision you made yesterday. Have you seen the TV program *Early Edition*? The star of the program gets tomorrow's newspaper today, and that's very helpful. He knows what is going to happen tomorrow, and he spends the whole show preventing it from occurring. Because he can see the future, he can change the future. It's like having a crystal ball. But in the real world, people can't use knowledge acquired after the fact to help them with decisions they had to make earlier. This has to do with an extremely important concept called *hindsight bias*.

Hindsight-biased thinking is a thinking error that leads to faulty beliefs about how much knowledge you possessed before negative outcomes were known—your beliefs about what you knew before outcomes were known. *Hindsight bias* is a term you will want to engrave in your memory. Read the next paragraph out loud.

Hindsight bias occurs when information obtained after an event distorts or biases a person's memory of what he or she knew before the event occurred. Hindsight bias is akin to "Monday morning quarterbacking" and is implied by statements such as "I should have known better," " I should have done something differently," "I saw it coming," "I knew what was going to happen" (before outcomes were known), and "I could have prevented it." As applied to trauma, many survivors falsely believe that the events were foreseeable—hence preventable.

Hindsight-biased thinking is also signaled by phrases such as "There were warning signs . . . There were red flags (signaling what was going to happen) . . . There were hints or clues

I should have picked up on . . . At some level, I knew (I was supposed to leave) . . . I was in denial . . . I kept making excuses . . . I was kidding myself . . . I was rationalizing." Have you ever been to a funhouse and looked into one of the wavy mirrors that distorts your appearance. Hindsight bias is like that. Hindsight-biased thinking distorts your memory of what you knew before the outcome was known. It's remembering yourself as being smarter than you were capable of being—as if you knew something that you did not know and did not learn until later. It's like remembering yourself having a crystal ball, which you did not have.

Hindsight-biased thinking is extremely common among trauma survivors. But it isn't something that just trauma survivors do. Everyone tends to do it. And it has been demonstrated over and over again in studies with college students and other populations (Fischhoff 1975).

Generally, when good things happen, people say, "I knew that was going to happen," and they can take some credit. The feeling is positive. But when bad things happen, then it's trouble: "Oh my god, I could have prevented it! I could have avoided it. I could have done something. The signal was so clear."

Looking back, it looks like a big weed or a flashing red light. But, before it happened, it was just a blade of grass and no light was flashing. Fischhoff (1975) quotes the historian Florovsky (1969) as saying, "In retrospect, we seem to perceive the logic of the events which unfold themselves in a regular or linear fashion according to a recognizable pattern with an alleged inner necessity. So that we get the impression that it really could not have happened otherwise" (p. 288).

Cynthia's Story

Cynthia is a thirty-eight-year-old woman who was sexually abused at age twelve by her cousin's husband. Cynthia's therapist was having a hard time getting Cynthia to realize that she wasn't responsible for the abuse. Cynthia said, "I shouldn't have been flirting with him. I never should have gone into his room. I made him think I wanted it."

Meeting this resistance, her therapist took a new approach.

Therapist: Do you have any nieces or nephews who are about twelve years old?

Cynthia: I have several.

Therapist: Can you imagine a scenario whereby, if you molest one of your nieces or nephews, they could be in any way responsible for the molestation?

Cynthia: Of course not!

Cynthia didn't say anything for the next few seconds. Then, she said, "Do you know what I think I've been doing? I think I've been putting my thirty-eight-year-old mind in my twelve-year-old body." Cynthia was remembering herself as being street smart when she was still a very naive little girl. Anything having to do with sex was the furthest thing from her mind when she was teasing and kidding around with her cousin's husband. Cynthia's therapist then asked her if she would have gone into his room if she even had the remotest thought that he might molest her. "Never!" Cynthia replied. To which her therapist responded, "Well then, that's proof that you did not have the slightest idea that he was going to molest you. If an event is unforeseeable, it is not preventable. If you do not know something is going to happen, you cannot stop it from happening."

The Meaning of "Should Have" and "Could Have"

It may help to look at the meaning of *should* and *could*.

To say that you should do something means that you have an obligation to do something. A duty. A necessity. A responsibility. A job you are required to do. Something that you are supposed to do. That's the definition of *should*.

However, it makes no sense to say you should do something if you are incapable of doing it. You wouldn't say you should jump up and touch the ceiling if you couldn't jump. You wouldn't say you should go to the store and buy some milk if your legs were broken and you were chained to the bed. You wouldn't say that you should read a road sign telling you where to go if the sign was in a foreign language that you don't understand.

Should is the past tense of *shall*. *Should* implies power and capability. To say that you should have done something implies that you could have done something—that you had the capability of doing it. *Could* is the past tense of *can*. To say that you can do something means you have the ability or capability of doing that something. You could only have prevented something if you knew—in advance—that something was going to happen. You are only capable of preventing an event or outcome if the event is foreseeable.

Let's say that there is a minefield right next to you, and we tell you that you have to through it or we are going to shoot you. Now, if flags designate where the mines are, and you walk up to one of the mines, kick it, and it explodes, you would be able to say with accuracy, "I should have known better and could have prevented the explosion."

But what if we took all the flags away? You start very carefully tiptoeing across the minefield, and suddenly there is a big explosion. Would you be able to say, "I should have known better and could have avoided the explosion?"

Of course not.

Or, in another example, imagine yourself walking on a sidewalk next to a building. You take a right turn at the corner, and a mugger, who you don't know is there, hits you over the hand with a club and robs you. Were you capable of preventing this outcome if you had no idea there was a mugger waiting around the corner?

If You Had Known with Certainty What Would Happen, You Would Have Avoided It

If you knew with certainty all the negative outcomes that subsequently occurred when you thought you should have left, would you have done what you did—would you have stayed? If your answer is no, that is proof you did not know that this was going to subsequently happen.

Let us ask you this question in a second way. If you had known with certainty that all the outcomes that "could have been prevented" were going to occur, would you have stayed?

Again, if you said no, this is proof that you did not know what was going to subsequently happen.

We contend that there is no possible way that you could have known with certainty what was going to happen when you decided to stay. Otherwise, you would not have stayed.

Clear Thinking about Guilt

President Harry S. Truman was purportedly asked by a reporter in the late 1940s whether he had made the right decision in ordering the atom bomb to be dropped on two Japanese cities in 1945. If President Truman had been a "should've/could've" kind of guy, do you think he might have guilt over what he did, in light of the enormity of his momentous decision? You bet! Just imagine him viewing photos of the victims. He might have had some serious problems. But he didn't. He seemed to be doing fine. And the reason he was doing fine was clear from the way he answered the question. He said something like, "Knowing then—in 1945—what I know now, maybe I would have and maybe I wouldn't have made the same decision. I would have to give that a lot of thought. However, knowing today only what I knew in 1945, I would do exactly the same thing."

President Truman was able to distinguish what he knew when he made his decision from what he learned after his decision. His answer indicates he was able to separate what he knew then from what he subsequently learned and knew later. He was able to retain a healthy and realistic perspective about what happened that served to inoculate him from developing guilt. By the way, President Truman was a very decisive man. He might have agonized over his decisions, but once he made them, he never second-guessed himself.

The kind of clear thinking exhibited by President Truman is the kind of clear thinking you want to be striving for on all of your guilt issues.

Reevaluating the Extent to Which You Knew Better

Now we want you to look again at the first item on the AAGS: To what extent do you think that you should have known better and could have prevented or avoided the outcome? What is the correct answer? What is the answer that reality would dictate—that a panel of scientists would conclude is the correct answer?

a. There is no possible way that I could have known better.

b. I believe slightly that I should have known better.

c. I believe moderately that I should have known better.

d. For the most part I believe that I should have known better.

e. I absolutely should have known better.

At the end of this foreseeability analysis, most clients select option "a"—"There is no possible way that I could have known better." They realize that there was no possible way that they could have foreseen the negative outcomes. Otherwise, they would not have stayed. We hope you answered item number 1 the way most of our clients do after the foreseeability and preventability analysis.

Do You Still Think You Know You Should Have Left Sooner?

If you did not select option "a" in answering item number 1 on the AAGS, there is a good chance that you are insisting that you knew you should have left before that point in time when you indicated that you should have left—for instance, as illustrated in the following interaction:

Therapist: When did you first realize or learn that you shouldn't have married him?

Client: I knew that before I married him.

If you are thinking something like this, there is a good chance you are still engaging in thinking errors. You may still be remembering some unforeseeable negative outcomes as foreseeable—and therefore preventable. Consider the following therapist-client interaction:

Therapist: You're saying you knew you shouldn't have married him before you married him, but you did anyway. Was the abuse foreseeable when you married him?

Client: Yes! I knew better. My family didn't want me to marry him. And my older sister said that he had a reputation for having a really bad temper. I should have listened to them. I could have prevented the abuse.

Therapist: Then, why did you marry him?

Client: Because I loved him and thought we would be happy.

Therapist: Did you believe your sister?

Client: No. I didn't think she really knew him, and I thought I could prove my family wrong.

Therapist: If you knew he was going to abuse you when you married him, would you have married him?

Client: No.

Therapist: That's proof you didn't know he was going to abuse you.

The client was thinking she knew she shouldn't have married her boyfriend because she was warned not to marry him by her family. What she was failing to remember is that she did not believe her family; therefore, for her the abuse was not foreseeable.

Acting on hunches. Sometimes, women continue to insist they should have left an abusive relationship sooner because they had a hunch they should have left before they did or they actually went through a period of time when they actively considered leaving but decided to stay. After learning the negative outcomes associated with having stayed, some women "remember" staying as more likely or probable to have produced negative outcomes than leaving. Once we find out the outcomes of an event or series of events, there is a tendency to distort our memory of how probable the observed outcomes were.

Grace's Story

A woman named Grace thought she knew she should have left her abusive husband six months before she finally left. Grace said, "I knew I should have left him!" Grace said that she could remember to the day when she should have left. It was the day she started therapy, and her therapist told her that if she didn't leave, her husband was going to kill her some day. Grace said that she should have listened to her therapist and left him.

Grace had waited until her thirties to marry, and marriage was extremely important to her. During their courtship, her fiancé treated her like a princess, but he changed dramatically after they got married. She found his drastic personality change difficult to fathom and thought that his abuse of her was due to his drinking. If he just stopped drinking, the abuse would stop. Grace held strongly to the view that marriage is supposed to be forever, and she was committed to keeping her marital vows. In addition, her father was an invalid, and her mother had stood by him all these years. Now, it was her responsibility to stand by her man too. After all, her husband needed her, and the thought of him being alone made her feel sorry for him. Furthermore, she loved him, and she believed things would eventually get better. Moreover, Grace considered herself very intelligent and creative—eventually she would get it "right," and he would stop abusing her. If she left now, she would label herself a "quitter," and her son would be left without his father. Grace thought that, if she left, she might regret leaving for the rest of her life.

If we could get inside Grace's mind when she started therapy, she believed it was far more likely that things would get better than worse, and she had far more to lose by leaving than by staying. In addition and very importantly, Grace did not believe her therapist when she said that her husband would eventually kill her.

Well, in the next four months her husband continued to abuse her, and she was starting to run out of ways to get him to stop. About two months before she finally left, her doubts about whether the marriage would improve were increasing, but she still felt she had more to lose by leaving than by staying and trying to make the marriage work. Then, shortly before she left, her husband almost killed her. And this is when Grace had the following realization: "Oh my god, he's not going to change. I am incapable of getting him to change. Oh my god, my husband is capable of killing me. My son needs his father, but he needs a living mother more than he needs his father."

Grace's perception of the situation changed drastically based on what happened during the six months after she started therapy. Ever so gradually—based on a continuing stream of new information that she did not possess when she started therapy—Grace's perception of the likelihood that the marriage would improve changed until she finally lost all hope and left. She did not know, when she started therapy, what she learned over the next six months.

Emotional reasoning and using "gut feelings" as evidence. Every once in a while, clients will not conclude at the end of the foreseeability and preventability analysis that there was no possible way they could have known better. They say that "it just doesn't feel right" or "doesn't feel true." They may have been thinking that the negative outcomes were preventable for so long that they "feel funny" when they entertain the thought that the outcomes may not have been preventable. One client said that she had "gut feelings" she should leave but decided to stay instead, and up until now felt guilty for not acting on these feelings—because everyone told her "you should always listen to your gut feelings." And until now, she believed them.

When some but not all negative outcomes were foreseeable. Occasionally, clients continue to insist they knew what was going to happen because some of the outcomes were foreseeable—but not the really bad ones. They believe that the foreseeable outcomes were "signs" of the inevitability of the really bad outcomes. We will give you an example to illustrate.

Kate's Story

Kate knew her boyfriend had a bad temper. And she knew he had gotten into several fistfights with other people. It was foreseeable that anger was a problem her boyfriend needed to work on. Kate also knew that her family didn't like her boyfriend, and it was foreseeable that she might become estranged from her family if she married her boyfriend. But, did Kate know that her boyfriend was going to become physically violent with her? No. She believed that her boyfriend was trying to turn his life around, and she believed she could help him change. If anyone had asked Kate whether her boyfriend would ever become physically violent with her, she would have answered, "Of course not."

Reevaluating Foreseeability and Preventability One More Time

If you did not choose option "a" when you answered the first item on the AAGS, we would like you to read and answer item number 1 one more time: To what extent do you think that you should have known better and could have prevented or avoided the outcome?

a. There is no possible way that I could have known better.

b. I believe slightly that I should have known better.

c. I believe moderately that I should have known better.

d. For the most part I believe that I should have known better.

e. I absolutely should have known better.

If you did not choose option "a" this time either, we will not belabor the point. However, if you did not choose option "a," you may want to reconsider your answer again after we have completed the following justification, responsibility, and wrongdoing analyses.

One last thing about hindsight bias. Hindsight-biased thinking not only goes straight to guilt; hindsight bias is a thinking error that also contributes to other guilt-related beliefs. For example, hindsight bias contributes to faulty beliefs about "responsibility." If you think a negative outcome was foreseeable and you could have prevented it—yet you allowed it to happen—then to some extent you may conclude that you caused it. Of course, this kind of thinking involves another thinking error. Believing that you could have prevented a negative outcome is not the same thing as causing a negative outcome. One battered woman had insight about this when she said, "You're right. I didn't pull his fist into my face."

In our judgment, hindsight-biased thinking is the single most important factor that contributes to guilt, shame, low self-esteem, and the maintenance of PTSD and depression. If we had only one hour to talk with you, it would be about guilt. If we had only ten minutes, it would be about hindsight bias.

Take a Breather

You do not have to complete this entire analysis of guilt in a single "sitting." At this point, you may wish to take a breather and reflect on what you have learned so far before proceeding to the justification analysis. You may also wish to take breaks after the justification analysis and the responsibility analysis.

Analyzing Guilt—Part 2: Determining How Justified You Were for Staying

The most justified course of action in any situation is the best option, choice, or course of action among the courses of action actually considered at the time. For example, let's say we are helping you decide whether to move to New York or San Francisco. And you make your decision. Then, you come back three months later and tell us we gave you bad advice. "How is that?" we ask, and you say, "I should have moved to Miami." "Miami? Who said anything about Miami?" The most justified or best course of action had to have been moving to either New York or San Francisco because these were the only two options considered. If you had better reasons for moving to New York than San Francisco, going to New York would be the better choice and would be completely justified. If you had better reasons for moving to San Francisco than moving to New York, then moving to San Francisco would be the better choice and completely justified. You cannot compare moving to New York or San Francisco against another option that you did not consider when you decided where to move.

Two Important Thinking Errors

We want to talk about two major thinking errors that contribute to faulty conclusions about the goodness of reasons or justification for actions taken. These two thinking errors both involve inserting options or choices that did not exist when you decided to stay with your partner (and did not leave as you indicated you "should have").

Weighing the merits of actions taken against idealized actions which did not exist. The fantasy solution. Ideal or perfect courses of action that never existed as options cannot be used to evaluate your justification for acting as you did. You can't compare the goodness of reasons for what you did against ideal but impossible options or solutions that did not exist. Here are two examples of trauma survivors who compared what they did against ideal or perfect solutions that never existed:

A woman who was sexually assaulted and didn't fight back. "I survived," she said. "I wasn't injured. I should have fought back." After all, she wasn't injured. This woman is remembering herself as having been able to resist the assailant without risk—a fantasy solution that did not exist. Did the option of fighting back at no risk of getting hurt exist when she was being assaulted?

A woman who thought she should have been able to get out of an abusive relationship when the children were small—"somehow." This formerly battered woman, who felt guilty about not leaving an abusive relationship sooner, dwelled on a course of action that was ideal but did not exist for her. This is what she said: "I thought about leaving when the children were small. I should have somehow gotten my resources together and left. Somehow I should have been able to make it. But, when I sit down, I cannot figure out that somehow. It's like, why wasn't I brave enough to pack up and leave Hawaii? Why wasn't I the heroine? I used to daydream that I had packed up the kids and was gone to the mainland."

The tendency to insert ideal solutions as "options" may be partly due to our exposure to movies, TV programs, and novels where heroes and heroines routinely do the impossible—John Wayne, Superman, Wonder Woman, Xena the Warrior Princess. A recent example of a movie star doing impossible things was Spiderman, when the villain gave him the "choice" of either saving from certain death the woman he loved or a group of small children. It appeared that it was impossible for Spiderman to save both the woman and the children. Somehow Spiderman saved everyone.

Weighing the merits of actions taken against options that came to mind later. This is another thinking error. Options that come to mind later cannot be used to evaluate justifiability or goodness of reasons for acting as you did. Here is an example.

This is a true story. It was described in a journal article (Pitman et al. 1991, 18). A Vietnam veteran was undergoing reexperiencing therapy (prolonged exposure) in which he was asked to relive in his mind a traumatic event from Vietnam. His unit was being overrun, and he witnessed a friend being slain by the enemy. He was unable to save him because he was out of ammunition. As he reexperienced the incident, it suddenly occurred to him that if he had had the presence of mind to pick up a rifle belonging to one of the dead, he might have been able to save his friend. Preoccupied with his "presumed oversight," the veteran spiraled into a suicidal depression, thinking he could have saved his friend's life. However, did the option of picking up a rifle exist for him twenty years ago? Of course not. If that veteran were here today, we would ask him, "If you had even the slightest idea that you could have saved your friend's life by picking up a rifle, wouldn't you have done that?" And he might say, "Of course." And then we would say, "Well, then that's proof you couldn't have because if it had occurred to you, you would have." It was a theoretical option that did not exist in reality. For example, if you didn't know there was a door in the room you are in, you could not get out—even though there is a door.

Your Reasons for Staying in the Relationship (When You Previously Indicated You Should Have Left)

What were your reasons for staying in the relationship at that point in time when you indicated you should have left? Before you answer this question, here are some of the reasons our clients have given for staying with an abusive partner: "I believed I was obligated to keep my marriage vows . . . Divorce was not an option . . . I believed that the children needed their father . . . I felt sorry for him . . . I thought he needed me . . . I would have felt guilty that I abandoned him . . . I didn't have any money or anywhere to go . . . I was afraid of what he would do to me . . . He said that if he couldn't have me, no one would . . . I thought things would get better . . . I still had hope . . . I wanted to avoid the stigma of being a divorcée . . . My family would have blamed me for the breakup . . . I already had one failed marriage. I didn't want to fail at this one too . . . I would have labeled myself as a 'quitter' . . .

I was afraid that he would try to get custody of the children . . . I believed he would have killed me if I tried to leave."

Again, what were your reasons for staying in the relationship at that point in time when you indicated you should have left?

_____

_____

Alternative Courses of Action Considered But Ruled Out

What other options or alternative courses of action (if any)—did you contemplate or consider when you decided to stay?

1. _____

2. _____

Reasons for Ruling Out or Rejecting Alternative Courses of Action

For each "alternative" course of action which you considered, why did you reject or rule out that course of action? In other words, what did you think would have happened if you had you taken this alternative path (knowing only what you knew back then)?

1. _____

2. _____

Review your reasons for staying and for each alternative course of action that you contemplated but rejected.

Now, compare the goodness of your reasons for staying with your reasons for each of the alternative courses of action. What was the best choice among the courses of action that you considered at the time? In other words, for which course of action did you have the best reasons? (Note: If staying was the only course of action you considered back then—that is, you weren't considering leaving—you obviously had better reasons for staying than doing anything else.)

_____

Does it look as if the potential consequences associated with leaving were worse than those associated with staying? If you are like almost every client who has completed cognitive trauma therapy, you will have concluded that you had better reasons for staying with your abusive partner than for any of the alternative courses of action that you ruled out.

Below, circle the answer to item number 2 on the AAGS that you now believe to be correct. How justified were you for staying? (i.e., How good were your reasons for staying?)

a. I was completely justified in staying (excellent reasons).

b. I was mostly justified in staying.

c. I was moderately justified in staying.

d. I was slightly justified in staying.

e. I was not justified in any way for staying (very poor reasons).

If you had better reasons for staying than any other course of action considered, you should have circled option "a." The reason for this is that the best course of action in any situation is the best course of action among courses of action considered at the time. You were completely justified because you had better reasons for staying than taking any other course of action considered.

In a very real sense, then, the decision about whether to stay or leave may have involved weighing the pros and cons of staying with the pros and cons of leaving, and the option with the largest net benefit or the option with the least net loss was the best and completely justified choice.

Additional Thinking Errors about Justification

Sometimes, trauma survivors overlook benefits associated with actions taken. For example, by staying in an abusive relationship, many battered women validate a variety of "supposed to" convictions acquired while growing up—such as being true to their marital vows, fulfilling their obligation to stand by their partner (who "needs me"), being a forgiving person, accepting responsibility for making the relationship work, and keeping the family together. Leaving back then, when a woman still had hope, would have invalidated these beliefs and led to guilt. By staying, she revalidated her identity or obtained relief from guilt associated with the thought of leaving.

Trauma survivors also sometimes fail to recognize that in heightened states of negative arousal their ability to think clearly and make logical decisions is impaired. When women are trapped in an abusive relationship, they may be so hyperaroused from their PTSD that their ability to think rationally is severely impaired. A woman's tension may be so high that she is in a chronic state of confusion, unable to think logically or make rational decisions. In chapter 6, we gave you an example of a very intelligent woman who thought she should have left her abusive boyfriend much sooner then she did. But, when we analyzed her situation, she realized that she was so aroused and confused back then that she had to rock in a fetal position on her living room floor in order to fall asleep.

Comparing Your Reasons for Staying with Reasons for Leaving—If Leaving Was Not Considered

If staying was the only course of action that you considered when you indicated you should have left, we want you to compare what you did (staying) with the alternative course of action—leaving—that only occurred to you later.

Even though leaving wasn't perceived as an option—so was not available—let's put it in anyway. Knowing only what you knew back then, what would you have thought would happen if you had left? Assume that you decided to leave back then; what do you think would have happened (only knowing what you knew back then), and why might you have ruled out this course of action?

_____

_____

_____

Here are some answers that our clients gave:

- "I would have labeled myself a quitter."

- "I would have invalidated my belief that marriage is forever."

- "I would have invalidated my conviction that my children need their father."

- "I would have been homeless and in poverty."

- "I would have believed that I failed as a wife."

- "I would have to carry the stigma of being a single mother and a divorcée."

- "I would have invalidated my marriage vows."

- "I might spend the rest of my life regretting that I blew it with my first true love."

- "I would have guilt and shame for leaving someone who needed me."

- "I would have been risking my life or my children's lives."

Review your reasons for "staying" and "leaving." Knowing only what you knew back then, did you have better reasons for staying or for leaving?

_____

If you are like almost every client who has completed cognitive trauma therapy, you will have concluded that you had far better reasons for staying than for leaving. Look at item number 2 on the AAGS again and tell us what is the best answer. Knowing only what you knew and believed back then, what was the most justified course of action? How justified were you for staying? (i.e., How good were your reasons for staying?)

a. I was completely justified in staying (excellent reasons).

b. I was mostly justified in staying.

c. I was moderately justified in staying.

d. I was slightly justified in staying.

e. I was not justified in any way for staying (very poor reasons).

If you had better reasons for staying than for leaving, your answer will have to be "a."

Analyzing Guilt—Part 3: Analysis of How Responsible You Were for Staying

In an analysis of responsibility, we are concerned with what causes what; for example, what causes a pencil to fall to the floor? We are not interested in evaluating whether it's a good idea for the pencil to fall to the floor.

People tend to fuse or combine responsibility and wrongdoing—for example, when using the words "blame" or "fault." "Naughty boy. It's your fault for spilling the milk on the floor. You caused the milk to spill and you violated your good table manners of keeping the glass away from the edge of the table." Blame implies wrongdoing as well as causation. We will talk about wrongdoing later.

Most events have multiple sources of causation, though most people are unaware of the number of factors that cause things to happen. In other words, most events have multiple causes and very few events have single causes, but people tend to overfocus on contributing causes that are very near or right next to the final outcome or occurrence of the event itself.

Many of the contributing causes of events vary in distance from the final outcome along two dimensions—history and physical distance. There are historical causes and contextual causes that are removed in distance from the event or outcome. We will illustrate with an example.

Turn the room light off. Then turn it back on.

What caused the light to go on?

Your all-powerful finger? But who else? What else?

The switch . . . the wiring . . . electricity . . . electrons . . . light bulbs . . . the electrician who installed the switch . . . the person who paid the electricity bill . . . the contractor who built the building.

Who else and what else contributed to the light going on? If this room were on a small desert island, would the light go on? What are some contributing causes outside the room?

You might have said the telephone poles and the cables transmitting the electricity; or the power plant; the oil tankers or trucks that brought in the petroleum; the oil wells.

Petroleum or oil is fossil fuel. If there were no dinosaurs or other prehistoric life, we would not have fossil fuel to run the generators that make electricity. So this is a historical cause. Can you think of some other historical causes? Who discovered electricity? Who made the first lightbulb?

Who or What Contributed to Your Staying?

Now, we are going to help you identify what people, factors, forces—other than you—contributed to your staying in a relationship with your abusive partner. We have done this analysis with more than one hundred formerly battered women. Below is a list of factors that our clients have identified as contributing to their decision to stay with an abusive partner. Place a checkmark (✓) in the first blank space next to each factor that contributed to your staying with an abusive partner. At the end of the list, there are several blank lines where you can add additional factors that contributed to your staying with an abusive partner. After you go through the entire list, for each item you checked, go back and assign a percentage of responsibility. From 0 to 100 percent for each item, assign a percentage that shows how much each factor contributed to your staying with your abusive partner. Write the percentage next to the checkmarks designating each factor that contributed to your staying. Your total for the whole list is likely to add up to more than 100 percent—possibly much more.

  ✓   %

____ _____ My history of good times with my partner

____ _____ My socialization or learning history that taught me to believe that marriage is forever

____ _____ My minister or other religious authority who encouraged me to stay

____ _____ The fact that my mother was abused by my father, and she didn't leave him—that is, staying was modeled by my mom

____ _____ My socialization history that taught me "if you make your bed you have to lie in it"

____ _____ My partner saying that I promised him that I would never leave him

____ _____ Friends and relatives who encouraged me to stay

____ _____ My socialization history that taught me to believe that the children need their father

____ _____ My socialization history that made me very prone to guilt, allowing others to influence me by making me feel guilty

___ ___ My socialization history that taught me to believe that if the marriage doesn't work, I failed.

___ ___ My socialization history that taught me to believe that if someone apologizes to me, I am obligated to accept the apology and go back to the way things were—a fresh start, so to speak

___ ___ The abuse by my partner that resulted in my self-esteem going down so much I didn't think I deserved better

___ ___ My partner making me believe that I would never find another man who would accept me for who I am

___ ___ My partner's guilt trips that the children need him

___ ___ My partner's guilt trips that he would fall apart or commit suicide if I left him

___ ___ My social isolation

___ ___ My lack of financial resources

___ ___ My partner's abuse of me that caused me to develop PTSD

___ ___ My PTSD, which impaired my ability to concentrate and make rational decisions

___ ___ My partner's threats that he would physically harm me or the children if I left

___ ___ My naïveté or lack of knowledge about domestic violence (e.g., "I didn't even know I was a battered woman.")

___ ___ My socialization history that taught me to believe that all relationships are like mine

___ ___ My socialization history that taught me to believe that if I get out of this relationship, the next one will not be any better—maybe even worse

___ ___ My lack of knowledge about domestic violence resources, such as support groups or shelters

___ ___ My socialization history that taught me to believe that the violence was my fault (e.g., My partner always said, "Why do you keep making me do this?")

___ ___ My trauma history that resulted in my self-esteem going so low

___ ___ My socialization history that taught me to be so ashamed about the violence that I was ashamed to tell anyone

___   ___   The continued physical and emotional abuse that taught or caused me to believe that it would be impossible to get out of the abusive relationship

___   ___   My partner's threats that he would sue for custody of the children

___   ___   My partner's threats that he would harm my parents or other family members if I left him

___   ___   My socialization history that taught me that my partner would eventually change and stop abusing me

___   ___   My memory of how charming and wonderful my partner was at the beginning of our relationship

___   ___   Drugs or alcohol that clouded my judgement and my ability to make logical decisions

___   ___   My partner's pressure on me to use drugs or alcohol

___   ___   My partner's repeated apologies and assurances that he would change

___   ___   My child or children (who "needed" me to stay so they could be with their father)

___   ___   My dissociation or emotion-focused coping that prevented me from even thinking about how to get out of my relationship

___   ___   My socialization history that taught me to believe that I had to keep my promises

___   ___   Romance novels and movies that depicted heroines changing despicable men

___   ___   The social stigma of being a divorcée and single parent

___   ___   _____

___   ___   _____

___   ___   _____

___   Grand total percent

Reappraising Your Degree of Responsibility

After you have completed assigning the percentages, we want you to add them up and put the grand total at the bottom of the list. Are you surprised by the grand total? If you are like almost all of our clients who have completed this exercise, your total of outside contributing causes of staying will have added up to anywhere from 300 percent to 2,000 percent.

Now, we have a problem because reality dictates that the grand total cannot add up to more than 100 percent. When most clients first complete the AAGS on this issue, they considered themselves personally to be "completely responsible for staying" and considered themselves 100 percent responsible for staying. Let's say that you assigned external contributing causes 700 percent and assigned 100 percent to yourself. This adds up to 800 percent and means that 800 percent of responsibility for your staying has to be somehow reduced to a total of 100 percent.

You have two choices. You can either discredit all the outside sources of causation or you can reduce your percentage of responsibility. Please answer item number 3 on the AAGS once more: How personally responsible were you for staying in a relationship with your abusive partner?

a. I was in no way responsible for staying.

b. I was slightly responsible for staying.

c. I was moderately responsible for staying.

d. I was largely responsible for staying.

e. I was completely responsible for staying.

Your percentage of responsibility _____ percent

If you are like most of our clients, you either answered "a," that you were in no way responsible for staying, or "b," that you were slightly responsible for staying. If you assigned yourself any more than 20 percent, you are probably still exaggerating how responsible you were for staying in the relationship. If you identified sixteen external contributing causes, each contributing cause would be only assigned about 6 percent, on average, to add up to 100 percent. That would still make you seem pretty powerful, much more so than you probably were. Look at it this way. If any other woman had the same lifetime experiences you have had, she would have stayed too!

Additional Thinking Errors

If you assigned yourself more than 20 percent responsibility for staying, you may still be engaging in thinking errors that are causing you to exaggerate how responsible you were for staying with your partner. We will briefly discuss three of these thinking errors.

Confusing responsibility as accountability with causal responsibility—the power to control outcomes. There's a great job available. It pays $150,000 a year. Your job would be to make certain that every one of two thousand employees in our company comes on time and that not one single person leaves early. If we gave you that job, we could hold you accountable and fire you if anyone comes after 8:00 A.M. or leaves work before 5:00 P.M. But would you have the power to make certain that nobody comes late or leaves early—the power to cause people to come on time and stay until quitting time? The captain of the nuclear submarine that rammed a Japanese fishing vessel in the seas off Hawaii was discharged from of the Navy after the incident. However, did the captain have the power or knowledge to have been able to prevent the incident? Would the captain have allowed his submarine to ram the fishing vessel if he knew it was there? Of course not.

Emotional reasoning. We discussed earlier how emotional reasoning can occasionally lead clients to conclude that unforeseeable outcomes were foreseeable and preventable even after the foreseeability and preventability analysis. Emotional reasoning can also contribute to exaggerated or inflated perceptions after a client has completed the responsibility analysis. A woman may continue to accept a disproportionate share of responsibility even though she recognizes intellectually that such appraisals are inconsistent with the facts. She is giving more credence to her feelings than to evidence and logic. "Intellectually, I agree with you. But, I still *feel* responsible." As we said earlier, how responsible you "feel" about any negative outcome is simply not evidence that you were or were not responsible for what happened.

Existential beliefs about accountability that fail to take situational factors into account. Existential philosophy maintains that individuals choose their own destiny as a matter of choice or free will, and that individuals should accept responsibility for the consequences of their actions. However, this philosophy does not take into account the fact that most actions have multiple sources of causation, and the fact that situational and historical factors outside yourself can exert a powerful causal influence on what you choose to do. We hope you may realize that if someone else had exactly the same learning history that you have had, they would have done what you did when you "chose" to stay with an abusive partner.

Who or What Contributed to the Negative Outcomes of Staying?

Now, we want you to identify people, factors, and forces that contributed to the negative outcomes you thought you could have prevented by leaving—such as

- continued abuse of you

- problems the children are having because of their exposure to violence

- your lowered self-esteem

- your overuse of alcohol or drugs

- your becoming violent too

- your giving into your partner's pressure to engage in unwanted types of sex

- your guilt and shame for not having left sooner

Below is a list of factors that our clients have identified as contributing to these negative outcomes. Place a checkmark (✓) next to each factor that causally contributed to your continued abuse. At the end of the list, there are several blank lines where you can add factors that contributed to your continued abuse and other problems that occurred as a result of having stayed. After you go through the entire list, go back and, for each item you checked, assign a percentage of responsibility. From 0 to 100 percent, assign a percentage that shows how much each factor contributed to these problems. Write the percentage next to the checkmarks.

✓	%	
___	___	My partner, who inflicted the abuse.
___	___	My partner's prior trauma history that made him a cold, callous person capable of criminally violating my rights
___	___	My partner's exposure to family violence while growing up
___	___	My partner's mother not protecting him from his father's wrath—resulting in him learning to hate women
___	___	Alcohol and/or drugs that increased the likelihood or severity of my partner's violence
___	___	Overuse of alcohol and/or drugs that resulted in lowering my self-esteem
___	___	_____
___	___	_____
___	___	_____
	___	Grand total percent

Reappraising Your Degree of Responsibility

After you have assigned the percentages, add up the percentages and put the grand total at the bottom of the list. Then answer the second version of item number 3 on the AAGS: How personally responsible were you for causing the negative outcomes or consequences that were associated with staying with your abusive partner?

a. I was in no way responsible for the negative consequences associated with staying.

b. I was slightly responsible for the negative consequences associated with staying.

c. I was moderately responsible for the negative consequences associated with staying.

d. I was largely responsible for the negative consequences associated with staying.

e. I was completely responsible for the negative consequences associated with staying.

Your percentage of responsibility _____ percent

What did you learn from completing the responsibility analysis?

Analyzing Guilt—Part 4: Analysis of Wrongdoing (Whether or to What Extent You Violated Your Values)

By the time we get to the wrongdoing analysis in cognitive trauma therapy, our clients' sense of wrongdoing is usually lessened to a considerable degree because they have now concluded that

1. The negative outcomes of staying were unforeseeable, hence unpreventable.

2. What they did was completely justified (compared to other actions they considered at the time and knowing only what they knew back then).

3. They were negligibly or not at all responsible for causing what happened.

What Constitutes a Violation of Values?

"Wrongdoing" is usually assigned as a label when someone intentionally causes foreseeable harm. A person deliberately violates societal values, causing harm or damage that is foreseeable.

Did You Violate Your Values?

1. Did you intend to cause the negative outcomes or consequences that were associated with your staying with your abusive partner (such as the continuing abuse)? Yes _____ No _____

2. Did you know these negative outcomes were going to occur when you decided to stay? Yes _____ No _____

You see that wrongdoing does not apply to you. Sorry. Not guilty. Case dismissed.

A common thinking error that contributes to distorted conclusions about perceived violation of values is the tendency to draw conclusions on the basis of a tragic negative outcome rather than on the basis of your intentions before outcomes were known. In other words, people tend to conclude that they erred on the basis of an (unintended) negative outcome rather than to evaluate the morality of their actions based on intentions, or what they were trying to accomplish before the outcome was known. Hindsight bias is usually implicated when this thinking error is made.

Confusing accountability with the power to control or prevent negative outcomes. The same thinking error that leads to faulty conclusions about responsibility can also contribute to exaggerated perceptions of wrongdoing. For example, many parents of children who died suddenly because of an accident or sudden infant death syndrome believe it was their job to prevent harm to their children and believe they failed in discharging their parental responsibility.

Failure to see that the least bad choice is a moral choice. A common thinking error contributing to faulty conclusions about wrongdoing involves assigning a label of wrongdoing on the basis of absolute standards without considering the context in which the negatively judged action occurred. The thinking error involved here is the failure to realize that when all available courses of action have negative consequences, the least bad choice—the course of action with the least negative consequences—is a highly moral choice. We will give you several examples of trauma survivors who found themselves in situations where there were no unequivocally good choices available.

John's Story

John was an army medic during the Vietnam War, stationed near the demilitarized zone separating North and South Korea. John had enlisted in the army because he was very patriotic but chose to be a medic because he was a pacifist and opposed to killing. Early one morning, John's entire unit was awakened and told that some North Koreans were trying to sneak into South Korea to assassinate the president of South Korea. The unit was taken to the beach, and someone handed John a handgun to carry. As they stood on the beach, three submarines started emerging from the ocean. Someone climbed out of one of the subs in shallow water and started shooting. Everyone on the beach started yelling at John to "Shoot! Shoot!" John looked the other way, closed his eyes, and fired. The bullet hit the enemy soldier in his forehead, and he died instantly. John was then told to search the body and found a picture of the man, a beautiful woman, and a small child.

Much later, in therapy for PTSD, John was trying to cope with his sense of guilt. Whenever he spoke of the incident, he began to weep. He was also angry at his parents for raising him as a devout Catholic and for believing so strongly in the commandment "Thou shalt not kill."

John's therapist probed for more details:

Therapist: Were there many other Americans there?

John   There were several.

Therapist: Were they close by?

John: Oh yeah. They were right behind me.

Therapist: Oh. Then other Americans could have been killed.

John paused for a moment and then said insightfully, "I see what you mean." He had not realized until that very moment that the option of no one dying did not exist. John had also failed to realize that by killing the North Korean, he had validated his value that he was a patriotic American and the lives of his buddies were more important than the life of a hostile North Korean who was trying to kill Americans. By killing the North Korean, John selected the least bad choice—which was a moral choice and completely justified.

Veronica's Story

Veronica felt guilty about not disclosing her molestation by an adult neighbor when she was a preteen. During the wrongdoing analysis, her therapist described the thinking error of failing to realize that when all courses of action have negative consequences, the least bad choice is a highly moral choice. Veronica's therapist pointed out that disclosing the molestation was also fraught with a multiplicity of perceived negative consequences—including family disruption, getting blamed for the molestation, and public humiliation.

Three years before entering therapy, Veronica had been forced to make a choice between having custody of one of her two children or risking the loss of both of her children. Veronica had a son and a daughter—now ten and twelve years old, and she had fought for custody of her children with her ex-husband for several years. She eventually got custody of her daughter, and her ex-husband got custody of her son. Veronica's son sobbed at the thought of being separated from his mother and begged her to let him stay with her. The only way for this to be possible would be to go back to court, but if Veronica did this, she would run the risk of losing custody of both of her children. And her husband had much greater financial resources than she had.

Veronica felt that the risk was too great and told her son that he had to go live with his father. She was guilt ridden as her son tearfully boarded the plane to go live with his father. Veronica later discovered that her ex-husband mistreated his son while under his custody, which exacerbated her sense of guilt. In therapy, Veronica realized that she had not had the simple option of getting custody of both children. And knowing only what she knew back then, she had made the least bad choice, one which was completely justified and highly moral, given the circumstances at the time. Veronica realized for the first time that an unambiguously positive choice was never available to her. (Incidentally, both Veronica's daughter and son now live with her.)

Inflating the seriousness of a minor moral violation when the minor violation leads to an unforeseeable trauma. Sometimes, people blame themselves for a tragic outcome because they did something wrong that inadvertently led to the tragic outcome.

Alice's Story

Alice was a high school junior who was infatuated with her new boyfriend Alex, who was five years older. It was a beautiful day, and Alex suggested that she play hooky from school so they could spend the day bodysurfing at Sandy Beach on the island of Oahu. On the way, Alex said that he had to stop and get something at his apartment. Alice went in with Alex, and it was then that he forcibly raped her. Now thirty years old, Alice has been beating herself up for years: "I knew I shouldn't have cut school. I knew it was wrong. I wouldn't have been raped if I had just done what I was supposed to do."

Alice considered playing hooky from school that day to be an extreme violation of her values. She was elevating the status of cutting school one day from a moral misdemeanor (a minor moral violation) to the status of a moral felony (a major transgression) because her original action was linked to a tragic outcome— loss of her virginity to a sociopathic assailant.

If Alice (as a teen) had a great time at the beach and developed a positive romantic relationship with her then friend, playing hooky that day may have assumed little or no significance—the point being that the rape was unforeseeable; and, if the rape had been foreseeable, Alice wouldn't have cut school that day.

Reappraising Your Degree of Wrongdoing

Now, we would like you to reappraise your beliefs as to whether you violated your values for having stayed with your abusive partner: Did you do something wrong? (Did you violate personal standards of right and wrong by staying in a relationship with your abusive partner?)

a. What I did was not wrong in any way.

b. What I did was slightly wrong.

c. What I did was moderately wrong.

d. What I did was very wrong.

e. What I did was extremely wrong.

What did you learn from engaging in the wrongdoing analysis?

Do you still think you should have left sooner? To what degree do you feel less guilty about this issue?

_____

_____

Analyzing a Second Guilt Issue

Now, we are going to walk you through an analysis of a second guilt issue, and this time we know it is an issue for you because you are going to identify for us an issue that you would like to feel less guilty about.

Below, we have listed some common guilt issues of formerly battered women, which may give you some ideas for selecting a second guilt issue to analyze.

- guilt about starting arguments or talking back

- guilt about your children seeing or hearing the abuse

- guilt about putting your partner's needs ahead of your children's needs

- guilt about raising your children without a father in the home

- guilt about not doing more to stop or prevent the abuse

- guilt about problems your children are having now that may be related to the abuse

- guilt about using alcohol or drugs

- guilt about having an abortion

- guilt about a rape or incidents of childhood sexual abuse

- guilt about the sudden and unexpected death of a loved one (for example, guilt about not spending more time with someone prior to their death)

Completing an Initial AAGS for a Second Guilt Issue

At this time, we would like you to complete an AAGS for the guilt issue we are going to analyze next. When you have completed the AAGS, we want you to analyze your answers to the first four questions.

Foreseeability and Preventability Analysis

1. What it is it that you should have known better?

_____

2. What are some of the negative outcomes that could have been prevented?

_____

3. What is it that you should have done differently?

_____

4. When did you first realize or learn that this was what you were supposed to do?

_____

Now let's examine your answers. Once again, you cannot use knowledge acquired after making a decision to guide your earlier decision making. You can't use knowledge that you acquire on Wednesday to help you make a decision two days earlier on Monday. Finding out that the stock market went up on Wednesday cannot be used to help you make an investment decision two days earlier, on Monday.

If you knew with certainty what was going to happen when you did what you did, would you have done what you did? Assuming the answer is no, this is proof you did not know that was going to happen. We would maintain there is no possible way that you knew what was going to happen when you did what you did. Otherwise, you would not have done what you did.

Now, answer item number 1 on the AAGS again, below:

To what extent do you think that you should have known better and could have prevented or avoided the outcome?

a. There is no possible way that I could have known better.

b. I believe slightly that I should have known better.

c. I believe moderately that I should have known better.

d. For the most part I believe that I should have known better.

e. I absolutely should have known better.

If you did not select option "a" in answering item number 1 on the AAGS, there is a good chance that you are still "remembering" some unforeseeable outcomes as foreseeable. What were some of the negative outcomes that you think you could have prevented? For each of these outcomes, was this outcome foreseeable when you did what you said you should not have done?

_____

If you said no to any of these outcomes, there is no possible way that you could have prevented them. Otherwise, you wouldn't have done what you did. Again, if an event's outcome is not foreseeable, it is not preventable. If you don't know something is going to happen, you can't stop it from happening.

Justification Analysis

1. What were your reasons for doing what you did?

_____

_____

2. What alternative courses of action (if any)—did you contemplate or consider (but rule out) at that time?

    a. _____

    b. _____

3. Why did you reject or rule out each alternative course of action? In other words, what did you think would happen if you had taken each alternative path (knowing only what you knew back then)?

    a. _____

    b. _____

4. Review your reasons for what you did and for each alternative course of action that you contemplated but rejected.

    Now, compare the soundness of your reasons for what you did with your reasons for each of the alternative courses of action. What was the best choice among the courses of action that you considered at the time? In other words, for which course of action did you have the best reasons?

_____

Doesn't it sound as if you had better reasons for doing what you did than for any of the alternative courses of action which you rejected or ruled out?

Circle the answer to item number 2 on the AAGS (shown below) which you now believe to be correct: How justified was what you did? (How good were your reasons for doing what you did?)

a. What I did was completely justified (excellent reasons).

b. What I did was mostly justified.

c. What I did was moderately justified.

d. What I did was slightly justified.

e. What I did was not justified in any way (very poor reasons).

If you had better reasons for what you did than any other course of action considered, by definition you should have circled option "a." The reason for this is that the best course of action in any situation is the best course of action among those considered at the time.

Thus, the best course of action is completely justified—because the bottom line is, you had better reasons for doing what you did than any other course of action you considered.

Responsibility Analysis

What people, factors, and forces other than you contributed to the negative outcomes associated with this guilt issue? Write down or briefly describe each external source of causation (outside of yourself). Then, assign a percentage of responsibility to each outside contributing cause that you identified. From 0 to 100 percent, how much was each of these factors responsible for causing the negative outcomes associated with this guilt issue? Then add up the percentages.

%

_____   ____

_____   ____

_____   ____

_____   ____

_____   ____

_____   ____

_____   ____

_____   ____

_____   ____

Grand total percent: _____

Reappraise your degree of responsibility by answering item number 3 on the AAGS: How personally responsible were you for causing the negative outcomes associated with this guilt issue?

a. I was in no way responsible for causing what happened.

b. I was slightly responsible for causing what happened.

c. I was moderately responsible for causing what happened.

d. I was largely responsible for causing what happened.

e. I was completely responsible for causing what happened.

Your percentage of responsibility _____ percent

Wrongdoing Analysis

1. Did you intend to cause the negative outcome(s) associated with this event? Yes _____ No _____

2. Did you know what the outcome(s) would be when you did what you did? Yes _____ No _____

3. If all available courses of action had negative consequences, did you select the "least bad" course of action?   Yes _____ No _____

(Remember that, when all available courses of action have negative consequences, the least bad choice is a highly moral choice.)

4. Now, reappraise your beliefs as to whether you violated your values by answering item number 4 on the AAGS: Did you do something wrong? (Did you violate personal standards of right and wrong by what you did?)

   a. What I did was not wrong in any way.

   b. What I did was slightly wrong.

   c. What I did was moderately wrong

   d. What I did was very wrong.

   e. What I did was extremely wrong.

   What did you learn from the analysis of this guilt issue?

   _____

   _____

   _____

   _____

   Overall, what did you learn from this chapter?

   _____

   _____

   _____

   _____

CHAPTER 11

"Supposed to" Beliefs That Lead Women to Stay or Go Back

The process of female socialization involves teaching young girls a myriad of "supposed to" beliefs as guidelines or values for determining what is appropriate and inappropriate behavior. "Supposed to" beliefs are moral codes in certain respects—not unlike the Ten Commandments. Their validity, accuracy, or truth is never questioned or challenged—they are simply assumed to be true. For example, many girls are taught that they are always supposed to be polite, nice, and forgiving, which also means they are not supposed to be rude or selfish (which may be defined by elders as placing their needs ahead of anyone else's—that other people's needs are more important than theirs are).

Many "supposed to" values become inflexible expectations, and women try to live in accordance with these values in order to confirm their self-concept or identity as a woman. When they act in ways that are consistent with these values, women reconfirm who they are. When women act or contemplate acting in ways that are inconsistent with "supposed to" beliefs, they feel guilty and lose part of their identity. For example, if a woman for whom being nice is a strong self-expectation acts in a way she considers to be rude or unladylike, she will experience guilt and invalidate part of her concept of the kind of woman she aspires to be.

Challenging Your Guiding Fictions

Many "supposed to" beliefs that are taught to female children—and which they carry into adulthood—are guiding fictions which lead women to believe they are obligated to act in ways that are contrary to their best interests. In particular, female children are taught many guiding fictions that lead them to do the bidding of men and keep them in subordinate relationships with men. Historically, men have been viewed as being more important than women, who were viewed by many men as a "less than" gender. For example, until recently, men were always considered the head of the household. Even now, some women accept this particular fiction as true—and to the extent that they act in ways that are consistent with this fiction, they may tolerate mistreatment from their male partners.

We have identified nine "supposed to" beliefs or guiding fictions that lead many battered women to stay with or return to an abusive partner. In cognitive trauma therapy, we engage clients in an exercise that involves challenging fictional "supposed to" beliefs. In this chapter, we are going to ask you to examine and challenge these fictions the same way.

Challenging Guiding Fictions or "Supposed to" Beliefs

We will present each guiding fiction or "supposed to" statement, followed by a challenge to the accuracy, validity, or truth of the statement. We will ask you whether you have ever believed the "supposed to" statement to be true, and we will ask you which of the two statements makes more sense—the "supposed to" statement or the challenge. Then, we will elaborate on reasons why the "supposed to" statement makes no sense at all.

Each "supposed to" statement or guiding fiction will be noted with the abbreviation "GF." Each challenge will be noted by the abbreviation "C."

First Guiding Fiction and Challenge

Read the dialogue aloud.

GF 1:   You made your bed and you have to lie in it.

C 1:   Just exactly what does this phrase mean? You mean if I decide to do something, I can't change my mind?

Have you ever believed GF 1?   Yes _____   No _____

What do you believe now about the statement, and what do you think about the challenge? Which one of these two statements makes more sense? If these two statements were two sides of a debate, which statement would win the debate?

Did you make your bed today? If you did, does that mean you have to lie in it? Sounds silly, doesn't it? It's just a meaningless cliché with no evidence whatsoever that it is true.

And for every cliché that proposes some kind of truism, there is often another cliché that proposes the opposite. Absence makes the heart grow fonder. Right? But, what about out of sight, out of mind?

Many women believe that if they say they are going to do something, they have to do it, and if they promise to do something, they have to keep their promise. As one of our clients said, "After all, a promise is a promise!" That's just like saying, "You made your bed and you have to lie in it." A promise is a promise. Right, so a promise is a promise. What the heck does this mean?

Many women believe that if they make a promise they do not have the right to change their mind. For example, we have seen clients who stayed in an abusive relationship because their partner "held them" to their promise that they would stay with him forever. "You promised me," he said. "You can't break your promise."

Something important for you to know is that you can always reserve the right to change your mind. Changing your mind is your right. When you make a promise or commit to any course of action, that promise or commitment is based on the knowledge you possess when the promise or commitment is made. Based on new or subsequent information, the original promise or commitment may no longer make any sense. And if it no longer makes sense to keep a promise, it would be prudent to change your mind and commit to some other course of action that does make sense.

Let's say that NASA plans to send a manned spacecraft to a remote planet. Of course, the trajectory the spacecraft takes is crucial to the success of the mission. The decision makers struggle about what to do but finally make a unanimous commitment on the trajectory to use. "Yes, that is the trajectory we are going to commit ourselves to take!" But then, what if the spacecraft starts going off course? Are the decision makers going to continue committing themselves to the original trajectory? We don't think so.

Similarly, when you promised that you would never leave your boyfriend or husband, did you know how he was going to change and become a completely different person? Would you have made that decision or commitment if you knew that your boyfriend or husband was going to become psychologically or physically abusive? He is no longer the nice and charming guy he was when you said you would never leave. Based on new information, you would want to change your mind about any promise or commitment you made earlier.

Second Guiding Fiction and Challenge

Read the dialogue aloud.

GF 2: You have to keep your commitment to your marriage vows. Marriage is supposed to be forever.

C 2: Even though he broke his part of the marital contract over and over and over and over again?

Have you ever believed GF 2?   Yes _____ No _____

What do you now believe about this statement, and what do you think about the challenge? Which one of these two statements makes more sense?

One of the things that many women fail to realize is that vows are for two people—not just one person. In a marital contract—like any contract—both parties have obligations or responsibilities to fulfill. Otherwise, the contract may be considered null and void. Let's say you hire someone to remodel your home and agree to pay the person $100 a month to complete the work. And you pay the person $100 per month for six months, but the person never even starts doing the work. Are you going to continue to pay this person? Of course not. Because he or she did not fulfill part of the deal or contract.

Consider your marriage vows. Is this what happened? You said, "I promise to love, honor and cherish . . . through sickness and in health, for better and worse, till death do us part." And your partner said, "I promise to do anything I damn well please. I promise to lie to you, to swear at you, to slap or punch you, to cheat on you . . . anything I damn well please . . . till death do us part."

We don't think so. In certain respects, your marriage could have been annulled—to the extent that your partner never fulfilled his true marital obligations or responsibilities.

A person is only required to be committed to fulfill her part of any contractual agreement to the extent that the other party fulfills his or her part of the agreement. Why would a woman remain loyal and committed to someone who has shown no commitment to the relationship, has been repeatedly disloyal, and has treated her far worse than even a perfect stranger would?

Third Guiding Fiction and Challenge

Read the dialogue aloud.

GF 3:   You feel sorry for him, don't you? Therefore, you should stay with him (or go back to him).

C 3:   Even though staying (or going back) is not in my best interest? Even though staying (or going back) will not make me happy in the long run?

Have you ever believed GF 3?   Yes _____   No _____

What do you now believe about this statement, and what do you think about the challenge? Which one of these two statements makes more sense?

We would like to paraphrase strategy number 23 from the Self-Advocacy Strategies Questionnaire (see chapter 2):

If you say that you feel sorry for your abusive partner or ex-partner, you are making his problem your problem. If you feel sorry for him, you are supposed to do something about it. You are obligated do what he wants you to do—to go back to him or stay with him. Even if you don't like to see him suffer, it may be contrary to your best interests to do something that reduces your guilt and alleviates his pain. You are not responsible for solving the problems that he caused and for which he needs to be held accountable. Otherwise, he will never learn and will continue to mistreat other women the way he mistreated you. If you do something that he wants because you feel sorry for him, it means that you are placing his wants and interests above your own. Your greatest obligation is to yourself. It is important that you act in your best interests whether or not you feel sorry for him.

Fourth Guiding Fiction and Challenge

Read the dialogue aloud.

GF 4:   You should be resigned to live out your sentence.

C 4:   You mean I don't deserve to be happy!? How silly is that?

Have you ever believed GF 4?   Yes _____ No _____

What do you now believe about this statement, and what do you think about the challenge? Which one of these two statements makes more sense?

_____

This guiding fiction is less commonly thought than "you made your bed and you have to lie in it," but they mean essentially the same thing. We will tell you a story about a man who said he was resigned to live out his sentence.

Paul's Story

Paul was the eldest son of five sons of a conservative Baptist minister. Paul said he knew about a week after he got married that it had been a mistake. But divorce for him was unthinkable because he believed it would enrage his father, and that his father would never forgive him. Paul said that he was "resigned to live out my sentence"—until one of his younger brothers got a divorce and "the world didn't come to an end" for him. Then, Paul got a divorce and realized the folly of believing that he was obligated to stay and suffer in a bad marriage.

Fifth Guiding Fiction and Challenge

Read the dialogue aloud.

GF 5:   He apologized. Therefore, you should accept his apology and go back to the way things were—a fresh start so, to speak.

C 5:   You mean I can't accept someone's apology and still choose to have nothing to do with him if it's not in my best interest to do so?

Have you ever believed GF 5?   Yes _____   No _____

What do you now believe about this statement, and what do you think about the challenge? Which one of these two statements makes more sense?

_____

Beliefs about apologies have kept many battered women in abusive marriages. It's a big "supposed to": Turn the other cheek. Millions of women have stayed in or returned to an abusive relationship because they thought they were obligated to accept their partners' apologies and act as if the mistreatment never happened—even though the apologies proved to be nothing more than empty or hollow words. Many, if not most, batterers apologize repeatedly and continue to engage in the same wrongful acts over and over and over again.

It is relevant here to paraphrase self-advocacy strategy number 13 from the Self-Aadvocacy Strategies Questionnaire—concerning apologies:

Just because someone apologizes to you for some wrongdoing does not mean you are now obligated to do what that person wants or go back to the way things were—whether or not you forgive the person. To forgive means "to pardon or release from punishment." To forgive someone does not mean that you are now obligated in any way to go back to the way things were. The phrases "forgive and forget" and "turn the other cheek" have no relevance for women who have been criminally battered by an intimate partner.

A governor can pardon a convicted criminal and release him from prison because the man is no longer considered a danger to society and it costs too much to keep him in prison. Does this now mean that the pardoned criminal didn't commit the crime? Does this now mean that the governor is going to invite him over for dinner? Of course not. And you can accept your ex-partner's apology and still choose to have nothing to do with him.

Sixth Guiding Fiction and Challenge

Read the dialogue aloud.

GF 6:   If you just try hard enough or get it right, he'll change and you'll be happy. If the relationship doesn't work, you failed.

C 6:   No woman will ever be able to "get it right" with a man who is incapable of having a healthy intimate relationship with anyone.

Have you ever believed GF 6?   Yes ＿＿   No ＿＿

What do you now believe about this statement, and what do you think about the challenge? Which one of these two statements makes more sense?

＿＿＿＿＿＿＿＿＿＿＿＿＿＿＿＿＿＿＿＿＿＿＿＿＿＿＿＿＿＿＿＿

The belief that divorce represents a personal failure has led countless women to stay with or reconcile with an abusive partner. One of our clients said, "I already had two failed marriages. I didn't want to fail at this one too."

Many batterers don't even have a good relationship with animals, let alone women. For example, it has been estimated that at least 50 percent of batterers mistreat or threaten to mistreat family pets (Ascione 2000).

Seventh Guiding Fiction and Challenge

Read the dialogue aloud.

GF 7:   It is your responsibility to make the relationship work.

C 7:   If two people are in a rowboat and each one has an oar, they both have to row to make the boat move forward. If only one person rows, the boat will go around in circles and not get anywhere.

Hearing this set of statements, one of our clients said, "I would just row harder," to which her therapist responded, "Then, I guess you would go around in circles faster."

Hearing this set of statements reminded another client of what happened to her: "We never went anywhere. And then he invited me to go on a picnic. We went to this forest preserve, and he kept jumping out from behind trees and scaring me. Some fun! Then, we went canoeing on the lake. After ten minutes, I realized we weren't getting anywhere. So, I looked around. He had a big grin on his face and was paddling backward! And wouldn't you know. I was in the front, leading."

Another client, who was considering going back to an extremely cruel partner, continued to insist that it was her responsibility to make the relationship work. She said, "The way I see it, fixing a marriage is just like fixing a flat tire. If you have the repair manual, you should be able to fix it."

This client's therapist then asked her to close her eyes and imagine the following scenario: "Imagine that the biggest problem in your marriage is that you have a car with a flat tire. You and your husband argue about this all the time. If you could just get the tire fixed, your marriage would be fine. But you don't know a thing about cars or fixing tires. Then, one day you see an ad for a new book on repairing tires for women who know nothing about fixing tires. You decide to order this repair manual. About six months later, it arrives, wrapped in unmarked brown paper. You unwrap the repair manual and start reading it. Your heart skips a beat as you realize, 'This is going to be a cinch! Anyone could repair a tire with this manual.' You excitedly go out to the carport, take the tire iron out of the trunk, pop off the hubcap, and start loosening the lugs. All of a sudden, your head feels like a tuning fork. Your husband has come up behind you and smacked the back of your head. Now, he has his hands on your face and is trying to scratch your eyes out. Now, he's tearing pages out of the manual and is trying to gouge the tire with the tire iron."

Now, we would like you to close your eyes and imagine that the above scenario is happening to you right now.

What are the chances that you would be able to fix the tire—even if you had the repair manual? No way, of course not! The moral of this scenario is that it takes two people working really hard to make a relationship work; however, it only takes one person to destroy a relationship. Similarly, it only takes one person to prevent a meeting from being productive. Have you ever been to a meeting where the disruptiveness of one person prevented anyone from getting anything accomplished?

Fictions and Challenges for Women Who Have Children

Read the following dialogue aloud.

GF 8:   The children need their father. Therefore, you need to stay (or go back).

C 8:   Do they need a biological father who mistreats me and them? Isn't it far more preferable to have a single-parent mother who is loving and consistent?

Have you ever believed GF 8?   Yes _____ No _____

What do you now believe about this statement, and what do you think about the challenge? Which one of these two statements makes more sense?

_____

This particular "supposed to" belief is not only embraced by many battered women, it is also imposed on them by society. For example, consider the following interaction between therapist and client as they address this fiction in this same exercise:

Therapist: So you believe the kids need their dad. They need their father. They need a male role model. You need to go back to him.

Client: Everybody says that. Even teachers!

Therapist: Even though he's a terrible role model? Even though the kids are exposed to all kinds of things you don't want them to learn—by watching the way he behaves and treats his wife—their mother?

Here's a related fiction and our challenge. Read the dialogue aloud.

GF 9:   You're obligated to keep the family together.

C 9:   The best situation is a two-parent home where Mom and Dad model healthy ways of resolving conflict. However, a stable single-parent home is far better for the kids than a two-parent home where there is domestic violence and a dysfunctional marriage.

Have you ever believed GF 9?   Yes ____   No ____

What do you now believe about this statement, and what do you think about the challenge? Which one of these two statements makes more sense?

_____

These last two guiding fictions send the same message—that the children need their father and an intact family, with both mother and father in the home. This is as fictional as it gets when Dad is abusive! Often overlooked by these two "supposed to" statements is the harm caused by exposing children to a violent father and a mother who tolerates the abuse by staying in the relationship. What are the female children learning? That if they ever get abused by an intimate partner, they are supposed to stay in the relationship? After all, Mom stayed. And what are the male children learning? That it is okay for them to abuse their girlfriends and wives when they get older? After all, Mom let Dad get away with it. And what are the children learning about how to resolve interpersonal problems and how to resolve conflict in a mutually respectful way? Unfortunately, little or nothing.

Lessons Learned from the Guiding Fiction Exercise

How many of the "supposed to" beliefs discussed in this chapter have you believed? ____ (Go back and count up the number of yes answers you gave when asked whether you have ever believed each of these fictions.)

Has completing this exercise helped you understand why you stayed with your abusive partner as long as you did? Can you see how many battered women remain trapped in an abusive relationship by these beliefs?

We have found that most of our clients in cognitive trauma therapy have benefited in at least three ways from completing this exercise:

1. Completing the exercise has helped them understand or explain why they stayed with an abusive partner as long as they did.

2. The realization that the nine "supposed to" statements are untrue has given them increased peace of mind that they made the right decision by leaving.

3. As a result of completing this exercise, clients became far less willing to allow other people—including authority figures—to impose "shoulds" or "supposed tos" upon

them. Instead, they look for evidence whether it is a good idea or bad idea to do what someone else says they "should do" or are "supposed to do" or "have to do."

Has this exercise in challenging "supposed to" beliefs increased your understanding of why you stayed in the relationship as long as you did?

_____

Has this exercise in challenging "supposed to" beliefs reinforced your conviction that you made the right decision when you left your abusive partner?

_____

Has this exercise in challenging "supposed to" beliefs increased your resolve to resist doing something just because someone else says you should? And to look for evidence before deciding whether it's a good idea to do something that others say you should do or are supposed to do?

_____

When battered women first contemplate leaving an abusive partner, they often experience guilt or the anticipation of guilt because they know that, if they leave, several "supposed to" beliefs will be invalidated. This negative emotion leads many women to stay in the relationship to get relief from guilt or the anticipation of guilt. When the net consequences associated with the abuse become overwhelming, they may finally leave, but when they do leave, they leave with guilt related to the invalidation of the type of person they thought they were supposed to be.

To the extent that you held these expectations of yourself and acted in ways that were consistent with these expectations, you may have been motivated to stay in an abusive relationship. To the extent that you continue to hold these beliefs after leaving an abusive relationship, you are likely to experience guilt. To the extent that you reject or discredit these beliefs, your guilt will diminish or dissolve.

What did you learn from this chapter?

_____

_____

_____

_____

CHAPTER 12

Assertiveness, Aggressiveness, and How to Take the High Road

Assertiveness is all about empowerment. Assertiveness is about social influence, about not tolerating disrespect, and about getting your wants satisfied. In this chapter, you will learn how to identify subtle forms of verbal aggression or disrespect, how to assertively respond to verbal aggression, how to effectively communicate your wants, how to refuse requests for your valuable time, and how to assert yourself in a stronger fashion when others are nonresponsive.

The assertive road. The honorable road. The superhighway of effective or influential communication. There are two communication "low roads." We see two low roads when individuals are in conflict. We see these low roads in couples counseling that is not working. One of the low roads is verbal aggressiveness—screaming, yelling, accusing, backbiting, being sarcastic, saying mean things.

The second low road may be very familiar to you. This low road is a second way to perpetuate conflict. It is conflict avoidance. Responding to conflict with passivity. Peace at all costs. Sweep it under the carpet. Have you taken this communication low road? Yes _____ No _____ If yes, how often? And describe how you have engaged in conflict avoidance.

_____

_____

Relationships "go south" when one or both parties in the relationship are unwilling or unable to directly address and communicate about problems in the relationship. And marriage counseling never works when at least one of the parties is unwilling to talk honestly about problems in the relationship.

Assertiveness vs. Aggressiveness

Assertiveness can be defined as expressing feelings, wants, or opinions in ways that respect the rights and opinions of others (Kubany, Richard, and Bauer 1992). The key word here is *respect*, and not only expressing feelings and wants in ways that are respectful. Assertiveness also involves respecting the opinions of others. Everyone has a right to their own opinion.

Aggressiveness is the flip side of assertiveness. Verbal aggression can be defined as expressing feelings, wants, or opinions in ways that disrespect or violate the rights and opinions of others. The key word here is *disrespect*. Putting someone down. Attributing negative qualities or negative intentions to a person. Telling someone how they should or are supposed to think, act, or feel. Ordering a person to do something you have no right ordering them to do. Attempting to impose your will, wants, or opinions on another person with no regard for the other person's feelings, wants, or opinions. Certainly, everyone knows that physical violence is aggressive, and so is profanity, and so are obviously degrading verbal expressions, such as "slut," "whore," or "bitch." However, verbal aggression has many subtle forms that occur in all human relationships—not just violent ones—when people are in conflict.

Being Assertive Is Not the Same as Being Selfish

We want to dispel the common myth that assertiveness in women is rude, mean, bitchy, aggressive, unfeminine, unladylike, or selfish. Assertiveness is none of these things. Assertiveness does not violate the rights of other people. Assertiveness is self-advocacy. Assertive people place a strong emphasis on getting their own needs met as a high priority.

When Someone Is Being Aggressive or Disrespectful

Verbal aggression violates universal standards regarding human rights and violations of human rights. These standards stipulate that all people deserve to be treated with respect. If someone speaks to you using aggressive or disrespectful language, that person is looking bad—it reflects badly on him or her and says nothing about you. That person is breaking the rules by speaking to you in a disrespectful way, and you do not deserve to be treated with disrespect.

It is essential that you be able to detect when someone is talking to you in a disrespectful way. Therefore, one of the goals of this chapter is to teach you about some of the subtle ways that verbal aggression is expressed. If you are able to detect when someone is talking to you in an aggressive or disrespectful way, you will be less likely to absorb the hurtful message and experience emotional pain. The hurtful message will be more likely to bounce off as you realize that you do not deserve to be talked to this way. Furthermore, conflict is never resolved when people resort to aggressive styles of communication.

We are going to teach you effective ways of dealing with the disrespectful words that come out of other people's mouths. Once you have identified that a person has spoken to you in an aggressive or disrespectful way, you can respond in a way that neutralizes the disrespect and doesn't make you feel bad. More about this a little later.

The Assertiveness Movement and "I Messages"

The assertiveness movement reached its height of popularity in the 1970s. There were several books written on the subject, primarily directed at women, and workshops on assertiveness were commonplace.

Nothing has characterized the assertiveness movement more than the emphasis on communicating with "I messages." For example, "I'm feeling frustrated that we never do anything that I want to do. I would really like it if we did something I want to do this weekend."

The importance of communicating with "I" has been directly compared with aggressive communication using "you messages," which have been widely frowned upon. For example, "You're frustrating me. You won't do anything I want you to do. Why don't you care about my needs?"

The problem is that some kinds of "I messages" are neither assertive nor effective. While some "I messages" are respectful and positively influential, other "I messages" are neither.

Challenging Traditional Views of Assertiveness

Many books on assertiveness recommend some ways of communicating—in the name of assertiveness—that are actually quite hostile and likely to evoke anger and antagonism rather than empathy and cooperation (Baer 1976). For example, many assertiveness advocates encourage people to express anger as long as the anger is expressed with an "I message" (Jakubowski and Lange 1978). They have assumed that expressing anger with "I messages" will be as positively influential as communication of any negative emotion, such as frustration or hurt feelings. On the other hand, research on anger suggests that expressions of anger may evoke hostility and antagonism, no matter how the anger is expressed. In other words, research suggests that expressions of anger will instill anger in the person addressed and will automatically instigate or trigger a hostile response (Berkowitz 1973).

Let's take a closer look at anger and how it differs from distress (hurt feelings, anxiety, disappointment). Anger is a negative emotional state, with an implication of hostility or antagonism. By contrast, distress is a state of suffering, sorrow, or unhappiness, with an implication of needing assistance. Angry people fight. They argue. They raise their voices and say mean and hurtful things. They also ruminate about how to hurt someone or see them suffer. Therefore, expressions of anger are aggressive—not assertive—no matter how the anger is expressed.

"I Messages" vs. "You Messages"

We conducted four studies to assess the social impact of communicating anger and "you messages" (Kubany et al. 1995b). In each study, we asked subjects to imagine they were having a disagreement with their spouse or other intimate partner. Then, subjects were asked how they would react to several statements spoken by their partner. Each statement was presented on a separate page of a booklet. First, subjects were asked to rate how sympathetic and how angry the statement would make them feel. Then, they were asked to rate how likely they were to respond in a conciliatory way (to speak calmly or suggest a solution) or in an antagonistic way (to raise their voice or say something hostile).

Subjects rated their reactions to sixteen different statements of negative feelings. Half the statements were expressed with an "I message," and the other half were expressed as accusatory "you messages." Here are a few of the "I messages": "I'm frustrated . . . My feelings are hurt . . . I feel anxious . . . I'm getting upset."

And here are a few of the "you messages": "You're frustrating me . . . You're hurting my feelings . . . You're making me feel anxious . . . You're upsetting me."

Which set of statements do you think participants responded to more negatively?

In every case, participants responded more negatively to the "you messages." In this part of the study, we merely demonstrated the obvious.

The sixteen statements also differed in a second way. Half the statements were expressions of distress, and half the statements were expressions of anger. Here are a few of the expressions of distress: "I'm frustrated . . . My feelings are hurt . . . I feel anxious . . . I'm getting upset." And here are a few of the expressions of anger: "I'm pissed off . . . I'm angry . . . I'm getting mad . . . I am feeling resentful."

Which set of statements do you think subjects responded to more negatively?

When the statements were expressions of anger, participants rated the "I messages" of anger just as negatively as they did the "you messages." Interestingly, accusatory statements of distress ("You're hurting my feelings") had the same social impact as "I messages" of anger. Expressions of distress softened the impact of "you," while expressions of anger hardened the impact of "I." Of course, the statements that were responded to with the most anger and the most antagonism were the accusatory expressions of anger ("You piss me off").

We have consistently found that expressing anger is likely to evoke an antagonistic reaction no matter how the anger is expressed—whether as an "I message" or as a "you message." "I messages" that convey anger and hostility are aggressive, and anger expressed in any way is negatively influential. In fact, any verbal message that conveys anger, hostility, or disrespect, or attempts to force or impose a person's views on someone else, is aggressive.

Three More Types of Aggressive "I Messages"

We have identified three types of "I messages," in addition to "I messages" of anger, that are aggressive and negatively influential because they evoke anger and antagonism. These additional aggressive "I statements" include: *aggressed upon* statements, *masked aggression*, and *scorn* or *character assassination*.

Aggressed upon "I messages" are implied accusations, which convey that the person addressed has caused harm to the speaker. Examples of such statements include "I'm getting screwed . . . I'm getting a raw deal . . . I've been duped . . . I'm being cheated . . . I'm getting taken advantage of . . . I'm being used."

In our research on the social impact of different kinds of "I messages," this kind of statement had approximately the same negative impact as "I messages" of anger (Kubany 1995). Both types of statements evoked more anger and antagonism than assertive messages of distress.

Masked aggression starts with an "I" but ends with a "you." Imagine yourself talking to a friend who says, "I just went to an assertiveness workshop and learned about the importance of communicating with "I messages." Well, I just want to tell you where I'm coming from. I want to tell you how I feel. How I think. I feel that you are codependent and in denial. And I think that you're a hypocrite."

Assertive? Of course not. In fact, these really aren't true "I messages," are they? The main statements are accusatory "you messages." In our research on the social impact of various types of "I messages," masked aggression "I messages" evoked ratings of much stronger anger and antagonism than even the aggressed upon and "I" anger statements. Masked aggression statements are "wolves in lambs' clothing" types of "I messages."

Scorn or character assassination attacks the very soul of the person to whom the statement is directed. Imagine that someone says to you, "I resent you . . . I don't trust you . . . I don't care about you ... I don't respect you ... In fact, I hate you." What would you say in response?

Would you be likely to do or want to do what the speaker wants you to do? Almost certainly not. Scorn statements evoke ratings of anger and antagonism—at the same high level as masked aggression statements. In our pilot testing of different types of "I messages," scorn statements evoked extremely aggressive reactions from seven graduate students and psychologists who were asked to respond to these statements.

How to Respond to Verbal Aggression

When someone talks to you in a verbally aggressive way, we strongly recommend that you focus your response on the aggressive style of the message. Do not get into a conversation about the issue being raised—the subject matter of the aggressive message.

Let's say someone says to you, "You don't know what you're talking about." The issue or subject matter of this message is whether you know what you are talking about. Refrain from getting into a discussion regarding the merits of the allegation. Instead, convey in some way that the speaker is talking to you in a disrespectful way and that you do not deserve to be spoken to in a disrespectful way. For example, you might say, "That's not a very nice thing to say," or "I don't deserve to be talked to that way." Or you might say, "Your saying that I don't know what I'm talking about does not mean that I don't know what I'm talking about." In other words, just because someone says something doesn't mean it's true. This type of response often puts an end to conversation on the topic.

How to Respond to Aggressive Questions

Aggressive questions are a subtle form of verbal aggression that most people have difficulty handling effectively. Here are a few examples of aggressive questions: "Why are you so defensive? ... Why are you in such a bitchy mood? ... Why are you so hypersensitive? ... Why are you angry? ... Why are you such a wimp?"

Typically, people respond to aggressive questions either defensively or aggressively. Defensive reactions, such as "I'm not being hypersensitive," simply invite further aggression—for example, "Oh yes you are!" And aggressive responses to aggressive questions—for example, "You should talk"—usually trigger more verbal aggression and conflict escalation.

Responding effectively to aggressive questions is actually quite easy—once you know how. First, let's examine the message that aggressive questions convey. For example, consider the question "Why are you so immature?" If someone asks you why you are so immature, haven't they concluded that you are immature and are now trying to get you to agree with them?

You see, aggressive questions are nothing more than accusatory "you messages" in disguise. Aggressive questions are accusatory "you messages" conveyed indirectly. In line with our recommendations about focusing on the disrespectful style of aggressive messages, what might you say if someone says to you, "You are so manipulative!"

_____

The point is to recognize the question for what it is and treat the statement accordingly. You might say, "That's not a nice thing to say," or "I don't deserve to be talked to that way," or "Your saying I'm manipulative does not mean I'm manipulative."

What might you say if someone asks you, "Why are you so manipulative?"

_____

Again, you can respond exactly the same way you would respond if someone directly accuses you of being manipulative. For example, you might say, "That's not a nice thing to say," or "I don't deserve to be talked to that way," or "Your suggesting that I'm manipulative does not mean I'm manipulative."

How to Respond to Aggressive Exhortations by People Who Mean Well

Friends and family of battered women and many health professionals are unaware that post-traumatic stress can be long lasting and may not dissipate with the mere passage of time. In their impatience to see a battered woman get back to "normal" once she is safely out of an abusive relationship, friends and family may actually make matters worse by how they try to help. For example, people close to a battered woman often exhort her to "get over it" with a variety of "you messages"—as if recovery from PTSD is a simple matter of choice. Here is a list of statements that many battered women hear from friends, family, and even therapists.

- "You should be over it by now."

- "You need to focus on today and move on with your life."

- "You're not going to be able to get on with your life if you don't put it behind you."

- "What's the matter with you? You've got to let go and quit talking about it."

- "You've got to snap out of it."

- "You need to start beginning a new life and pretty much forget about it."

- "Don't think about it. If you stop thinking about it, it will go away."

- "You're just hanging on to this and being morbid."

- "It's almost as if you don't want to get over it."

- "Do you enjoy being upset all the time?"

- "You have to stop wallowing in self-pity."

- "You need to stop feeling sorry for yourself."

- "You shouldn't feel that way."

Do these statements sound familiar? Which of these statements or other kinds of unhelpful comments have you heard from people "who mean well"? How often do you hear them?

People who make statements like these need to be told that their remarks are not helpful. Here are a few suggestions of how you might assertively respond to people who mean well but who make unhelpful remarks:

- "I know you mean well. But it does *not* help for you to say that."

- "I would appreciate it if you don't ever say that again. It doesn't help and I know you want to help."

- "If you never say that again, we'll have a better relationship."

If you have friends or family or a therapist who talk to you in this way, you may also want to ask them to read this section of the book.

The Importance of Not Tolerating Disrespect

You cannot control the words that come out of other people's mouths. You cannot stop people from speaking in aggressive and disrespectful ways. However, you can control your exposure to the words of other people. You can end the conversation, leave the situation, or end a relationship with someone who persists in treating you with disrespect.

A rule of thumb is if someone has said two or three unkind things to you—to each of which you responded assertively—that you advise the person you are going to end the conversation if they continue talking to you in a disrespectful way.

Practice Makes Perfect

In cognitive trauma therapy, we practice with clients making aggressive statements and responding to these statements in the recommended ways. The therapist and client take turns selecting and saying aggressive statements and responding with assertive statements. This role-playing or skill-rehearsal practice has helped many clients feel less anxious when aggressively spoken to and has increased their skill and confidence in responding assertively to verbal aggression.

We want you to do the same role-playing exercise with an intimate partner, friend, or relative. Take turns selecting and saying aggressive statements and responding assertively. Come up with a list of aggressive statements or use previous examples from this chapter. You can use the following list of statements to respond assertively.

- "That's not a very nice thing to say, and it hurts my feelings."

- "Your saying that I'm (a certain way) doesn't mean it's true."

- "I don't deserve to be talked to that way."

- "That's an unkind thing to say."

- "That's a hurtful thing to say."

- "That's a nasty thing to say."

- "I would appreciate it if you didn't talk to me that way."

- "If you're going to continue to talk to me this way, I'm going to end this conversation."

- "I would appreciate it if you could say that in a nicer way."

- "Could you please say that another way?"

- "If you never say that again, I'll be better off, and you and I will have a better relationship."

- "I know you mean well. But it does *not* help for you to say that."

Responding to the Style of Verbal Aggression Really Does Work

We have had many clients tell us that responding to the style of other people's verbally aggressive remarks has enabled them to take control of conflictual interactions that in the past would have escalated or left them feeling overwhelmed, cheapened, or depressed. For example, clients have told us that saying "That's not a nice thing to say," or "I don't deserve to be talked to that way," or "Your saying that doesn't mean it's true" has often left the other party speechless. These types of statements never provide ammunition for an escalation of verbal aggression. This way of responding really does work in terms of influencing the verbal behavior of other people and has resulted in many of our clients feeling greatly empowered. We believe that if you incorporate the recommended verbal strategies for responding to verbal aggression into your repertoire, you will find that they work for you too.

Your Use of Verbal Aggression

So far, the focus of this chapter has been on helping you identify and learn how to respond assertively in response to verbal aggression. However, we know that many, if not most, people tend to become aggressive when engaged in conflict with people who are being aggressive (Smith, Sanders, and Alexander 1990).

It is very important that you think about what you want to accomplish when you address conflict with anyone. If you just want to get the other person upset—and sometimes people do intentionally say hurtful things out of anger—you may choose to express anger and say things that are hostile and aggressive. However, if you want to influence the other person to do something you want them to do or to stop doing something you dislike, you are unlikely to accomplish this objective with verbal aggression. Instead, you will alienate the other person and invite counteraggression. In the next section, we will discuss the basics of assertive communication, which will increase the likelihood that you will get your interpersonal wants and needs satisfied and increase chances that you will influence other people in positive ways.

Assertive Communication Basics

By expressing feelings, wants, or opinions in ways that respect the rights and opinions of others, the focus is on you rather than on someone you want to influence. You will be "owning" your feelings, wants, and opinions and will not be attributing negative intentions or qualities to the person you want to influence. Communicating assertively does not guarantee that people you want to influence will do what you want them to do. However, it will increase the chances or probability that they will respond in a positive way. In addition, communicating assertively is unlikely to escalate conflict or fuel another person's hostility. In this section, we will cover the basics of assertive communication.

Saying No

It is your perfect right to say no. If you have a hard time saying no to people, you probably have a problem in all areas of assertiveness. Refusing requests requires a minimal response; yet, many women have a hard time turning other people down, even when requests are extremely unreasonable. If you have trouble saying no, under what circumstances do you have a hard time saying no?

_____

_____

There are at least two reasons why many battered women have difficulty refusing requests from other people. First, many battered women give in to other people's requests and demands because they say they don't like to hurt other people's feelings. Have you had trouble saying no because you didn't want to hurt a person's feelings? Yes ＿＿ No ＿＿

Actually, it is not hurting other people's feelings that is the primary problem here. The problem is that many formerly battered women are afraid that other people will get upset or angry if they do not acquiesce, and they do not want to be perceived as the direct instigator or cause of anyone's negative feelings.

Alma's Story

Alma was extremely unassertive and in psychotherapy. On one occasion, Alma told her therapist that a friend asked her to go to the beach, and she did not want to go. However, she agreed to go "because I didn't want to hurt her feelings." Her therapist then asked, "Well, how was it?" Alma replied, "Oh, I didn't go." She said that when she next saw her friend, she was going to make up an excuse about why she hadn't shown up and she would apologize profusely.

Here is clearly a situation where hurting someone's feelings was not the issue. Certainly, Alma's friend was far more upset with Alma because Alma didn't show up at the beach than she would have been if Alma had simply said on the phone, "I can't make it today." But Alma was afraid to say something she thought would result in someone getting angry. She got immediate relief by saying she would go to the beach, and her friend's wrath did not come until later. Alma got immediate gratification at considerable cost to the relationship with her friend.

How about you? If you have said that you don't like to hurt other people's feelings, isn't the real issue that you are (or were) afraid the other person would get upset if you turned them down?

A second reason many battered women have trouble saying no is that they would feel rude or selfish if they said no, which would cause them to feel guilty. Have you had trouble saying no because you did not want to feel rude or selfish? And, on those occasions when you did put your own wants first and said no, did you feel guilty?

How You Spend Your Time Is Up to You

How you choose to spend your time is up to you. No one else has a right to spend time with you or to make you spend time on their behalf unless you give your time freely. You have no obligation to spend time doing what someone else wants you to do, and you are not violating anyone's rights by turning down requests for the use of your time. Refusing to do something you do not want to do is a form of self-advocacy. Doing something for someone else at your expense is putting someone else's needs ahead of your own. If you don't put yourself first, who will?

The Importance of Being Able to Say No Without Giving Reasons Why

It is very important that you be able to say no without making excuses or giving explanations. This is important because people who put their wants ahead of yours will try to talk you out of your decision. They will try to get you to change your mind. Has anyone ever talked you out of your reasons for not wanting to do something and gotten you to say yes when you wanted to say no.   Yes _____ No _____

If so, briefly describe what happened.

_____

Turning down a request for a date. If someone you don't want to go out with asks you to go out with him, say something like, "That's nice of you to ask, but I can't make it." If the person asks you why you won't go out with him or gets pushy or applies pressure to get you to change your mind, repeat or paraphrase your initial response. For example, you might say, "I can't make it, but thanks anyway." If the person persists, escalate your response to something like this: "I am not available to go out with you, and I have to go. Good-bye." Then hang up the phone if you're on the phone. If you're saying this in person, you can just say, "Excuse me," and leave.

Turning down requests from friends and family. Many formerly battered women find it hard to stick to their guns and say no to friends or family, who often try to talk them out of their reasons for saying no. For example, a client named Bernice worried that if she just said "I can't make it" to her mother, her mother would get mad and probably stop talking to her. Two weeks later, Bernice's mother asked her to do something, and Bernice said, "I can't this weekend, Mom." And her mother answered, "Okay." At her next therapy session, Bernice expressed amazement and said, "Wow, I feel so empowered."

Turning down requests that you buy something. In turning down door-to-door salespeople and telemarketers, it is important to keep the interaction very brief. On the telephone, as soon as you realize it is a sales call, you might say:

- "I'm not interested. But have a nice day. Good-bye."

- "I'm not interested in buying anything. I don't want to take any of your valuable time. Good-bye."

- "I don't have time for this call. Good-bye."

Some people might think that this last response borders on rude. However, if you know that you are going to eventually say no, you are wasting the salesperson's time by staying on the phone with him or her. In fact, Congress has recently passed legislation that allows you to prohibit telemarketing on your phone, as it's considered an invasion of privacy. You are not rude to say no.

Refusing to disclose or talk about something. Some formerly battered women think that if someone asks them about something, they have to tell the other person what it is he or she wants to know. Remember, what is in your mind belongs to you and you have no obligation whatsoever to talk about any topic or tell a person anything. You might say something like, "I'd prefer not to talk about that. Could we please change the subject?" This also goes back to saying no without giving reasons why. Remember, your reasons for whatever you want to do (or not do) belong to you, and you have no obligation to disclose your reasons if you would rather not.

Saying No after You Said Yes

Sometimes, people agree to someone's request to do something and subsequently regret they did based on a consideration of other things they need to do or would simply rather do. We have already emphasized the importance of always reserving the right to change your mind after you have made a decision, based on new information. Let's say you agreed to help someone out on the weekend and later realize that if you help the other person out, you will not have time to do something you really want or need to do. We suggest that you contact the other person and tell them directly and succinctly that, "I know I said I would help you out, but I failed to realize how much I have to do. I will not be able to help you out after all." Or you might say, "I won't be able to make it after all. I've got some other things that I have to do."

Communicating Feelings and Wants

To get your needs and wants satisfied, you need to tell people how you feel and what you want. Other people cannot read your mind and will not know how you feel or what you want unless you tell them.

Communicating Feelings

Always communicate negative feelings as distress rather than as anger. Distress often evokes empathy and an inclination to nurture or help. Anger evokes hostility and antagonism. Here are a few recommended ways of communicating distress: "My feelings are hurt . . . I'm upset . . . I'm frustrated . . . I'm disappointed . . . I'm feeling sad . . . I feel anxious."

Making Requests and Communicating Wants

We recommend that you communicate your wants directly and specifically. For example,

- "I would appreciate it if we could go to a movie that I like tonight."

- "I would appreciate your not calling after 8 P.M. on weeknights.

- "I would appreciate it if you would give me a ride."

- "I would appreciate it if you would pick me up after work."

- "I would appreciate your not borrowing my belongings without my permission."

- "I would appreciate your keeping your voices down."

Communicating your wants this way conveys that the other person has the power to please you, and we believe that by communicating in this way or in similar ways, it will increase the probability that the other person will do what you want them to do. If the other person wants to please you and knows what you want, there is a good chance that he or she will do it. But, it is extremely important that you are explicit about what you want.

There are several phrases similar to "I would appreciate" for communicating wants in ways that convey to the other person that he or she has the opportunity to do something that would give you pleasure:

- "It would really please me if . . . "

- "You would make my day if you would . . .

- "It would really make me happy if you would . . . "

- "You would be doing me a big favor if . . . "

- "I would be grateful if . . . "

Many people express wants and make requests indirectly in the form of questions. For example, "Would you like to go to a movie tonight?" It is much easier to say no to questions than to direct expressions of wants, and questions are often misinterpreted or misunderstood. Having done years of marriage counseling, Dr. Kubany knows that many individuals in distressed marriages falsely assume that their spouses know what their specific wants are.

Assertive Escalation

Asking someone to do something is not a guarantee that your request will be granted. This circumstance may sometimes call for what we refer to as *assertive escalation*. Assertive escalation involves either a more forceful request or telling the other person what you are going to do (something the person may not want you to do) if he or she chooses not to grant your request. This "if . . . then" strategy is usually phrased in a couple of ways: "If you do not . . . then I will have no choice but to . . . " or "If you will not . . . I am going to . . . "

An example might involve asking a person with whom you are having a disagreement to please speak more softly. If the other person does not comply, you might then say, "If you won't lower your voice, I am going to end this conversation," and then end the conversation if the other person persists. It would probably be too strong to say you are going to end the conversation as soon as the other person starts to raise his or her voice, but this response is a reasonable and assertive course of action if the other person refuses to honor your reasonable request.

It is very important that you follow through on what you say you are going to do. If you say you are going to end a conversation if a person persists in being aggressive, end the conversation if he or she persists. If you don't, you will lose credibility.

Assertive Escalation in Child Management

Assertive escalation is widely advocated by child management experts for addressing noncooperation and other child behavior problems. For example, if a child refuses a reasonable request, parents may be advised to invoke negative consequences. For example, if a child refuses to pick up his or her toys, parents may be advised to tell the child that he or she can't watch TV until the toys are picked up. As an initial response, this might be a bit harsh, but not after a reasonable assertive request is disregarded. Once again, the standard phrase is "If you do that again, then . . . " or "If you do not . . . then . . . " For example, "If you talk to me that way again, then you are going to have to go to your room for five minutes."

Assertive Escalation in the Workplace

Assertive escalation can be an influential tool when there is interpersonal conflict in the workplace. Sometimes, conflicts between workers may continue unabated as a source of chronic stress, and sometimes people quit their jobs because of workplace conflict. Other times, employees will go directly over a coworker to the supervisor—without telling the person with whom they are in conflict. Unfortunately, this tactic will almost always alienate the coworker and do irreparable harm to that relationship. Instead, we would recommend saying something to the coworker like this: "As I told you before, I would really like to work this problem out with you at our level—just between the two of us. But, if we can't work it out, I will have no choice but to go to the supervisor."

To threaten to go to a supervisor at the first signs of conflict would be somewhat abrasive and might aggravate the conflict. After the coworker shows no attempt to resolve the conflict, however, giving her a choice regarding going to a supervisor would be appropriate and professional.

Sexual or other harassment in the workplace often calls for assertive escalation. Many unassertive women say little or nothing when they hear sexually inappropriate remarks. Unfortunately, there is some evidence to suggest that passivity may actually invite continued harassment and may even be a precursor to victimization or revictimization (Rosen and Martin 2000).

If someone at work makes a sexually offensive remark, which may or may not be maliciously intended, you may wish to overlook the first occurrence as a rare event, unlikely to occur again, or you may choose to respond with a low-level assertive response, such as "I would appreciate your not using that kind of language" or "That remark was offensive. I certainly hope you never say anything like that again."

When it comes to sexual harassment that is unmistakable, we recommend zero tolerance. If the first inappropriate remark is grossly inappropriate or offensive, we recommend an escalated assertive response right from the start. For example, you might say something like "That is sexual harassment. I will not tolerate someone saying that. If you ever say something like that again, I will have no choice but to report it immediately. I mean it." Similarly, if someone touches you in an inappropriate manner, you should let him know that if he ever does it again, you will report it.

Assertive Escalation in an Intimate Relationship

You can also utilize assertive escalation to promote your best interests in an intimate relationship. Let's say you want to do something you know your boyfriend usually wouldn't do—for example, go to a particular concert or a dog show. Ordinarily, you might just tell your boyfriend that you are planning to go the concert with a friend because you know he doesn't like this music. Of course, this might invite a response like, "How do you know what I like?" Instead, if you want your boyfriend to go with you, we would recommend that you ask your boyfriend to go first. Then, if he says, "You know I don't like that kind of music," you can say, "I understand. If you don't want to go with me, I'll just ask a friend to join me." Then if he says, "You would go without me?" you can say, "I'd rather go with you, but I would rather go with a friend than not go at all."

Here's an example of assertive escalation in a dating situation. Clara was having trouble getting her needs met with her boyfriend, who was not abusive but was quite selfish and self-centered. After her session on assertiveness in cognitive trauma therapy, Clara and her boyfriend went out for pizza. He wanted to order a combination pizza, and because she didn't like pepperoni, Clara asked if they could order the pizza with the pepperoni on one side. Her boyfriend replied, "What's the big deal? You can just pick it off." To which Clara replied, "You're right, it's not a big deal to pick off the pepperoni. It's also not a big deal to have the pepperoni on one side of the pizza." Would you rather have pizza with me tonight, or would you rather I go home?" Clara and her boyfriend ended up enjoying their pizza with all the pepperoni on one side.

Additional Important Benefits of Becoming Assertive

Research on self-efficacy indicates that people tend to avoid activities and situations they believe exceed their coping capabilities, but readily undertake challenges they think they are capable of handling (Ozer and Bandura 1990). Consistent with this research, there is evidence that assertive women interpret potentially stressful social situations as "challenging," whereas unassertive women interpret the same situations as "threatening" (Tomaka et al. 1999). Practicing and applying the skills you have learned in this chapter should increase your self-confidence in social situations and may directly lessen your levels of stress and symptoms of PTSD.

What did you learn from reading this chapter, answering the questions, and doing the role-playing exercise?

_____

_____

_____

_____

CHAPTER 13

Managing Contacts with Former Partners

The prospects of running into or receiving phone calls from abusive ex-partners is a source of considerable anxiety and even dread for many formerly battered women. What would you say if—out of the blue—your abusive ex-partner came up to you or called you on the phone?

_____

_____

Some common responses are "I don't know . . . I don't think that I will see him (I don't think he will call) . . . I'd freeze . . . I'd panic . . . It depends on what he said . . . I'll deal with it if or when it happens."

We are assuming that your relationship with your ex-partner is irrevocably over. In cognitive trauma therapy, we tell clients that if their relationship is over and they have no intention of reconciling, they should say the same thing no matter what their ex-partner says—that the relationship is over and there is nothing to talk about. For example, if your ex-partner tries to get you to reconcile with him or disputes your reasons for ending the relationship, there is still nothing to talk about because you have made a final decision. Any further discussion is pointless or a waste of time. Most batterers are extremely manipulative, however, and will rely on a variety of verbal strategies to influence their ex-wives or ex-girlfriends or to get them to change their minds about something. And if one strategy doesn't work, they will try something else. For example, they may be extremely complimentary. If that doesn't work, they may say that they can't live without their ex-wife. If that doesn't work, they may try to lay a guilt trip. If that doesn't work, they may raise their voice or say something verbally abusive.

Here are a few rules that will help you manage unwanted contacts:

- Carefully plan and rehearse exactly what you are going to say (even if it is unlikely you will see or be contacted by your ex-partner). And say nothing more than you plan to say.

- Keep the interaction as brief as possible. We're talking about a matter of seconds here, not minutes.

- Speak softly and slowly in a matter-of-fact way. If the contact is face-to-face, look him straight in the eye.

- Stay with your script. Say the same things, no matter what he says and no matter why he says he is contacting you.

What to Do If You Are Contacted by an Ex-Partner

In certain respects, this chapter is a continuation of our chapter on assertiveness. Remember from the last chapter—how you spend your time belongs solely to you, and your ex-partner has no right to your time. The bottom line is to not tolerate disrespect and to keep unwanted contacts extremely brief.

Face-to-Face Contacts

If your ex-partner approaches you in person, we recommend that you say something like the following: "Our relationship is over. There is nothing to discuss. Please excuse me." Then walk away.

If your ex-partner continues to follow and talk with you, you may choose to say something like, "If you don't leave me alone, I will have no choice but to . . . call a manager or security guard . . . scream . . . let the police know that you violated the restraining order."

Telephone Contacts

If your ex-partner contacts you by phone, we recommend similar ways of managing the interaction. For example, you might say, "Our relationship is over. There is nothing to discuss. Please don't call. I have to go. Good-bye." Then hang up. Again, try to speak in a matter-of-fact way and speak slowly, without raising your voice.

Sometimes an ex-partner keeps calling back in spite of a woman's declarations that she has nothing to say. If this happens, we recommend that the next time he calls, you say something to the effect that, "I have nothing more to say. Please don't call me anymore. If you call again and I hear your voice, I am going to going to hang up without saying anything." We recommend that you answer all subsequent calls in an upbeat or cheery voice and softly hang up if you hear your ex-partner's voice on the line.

What to Do If Contacts Are Necessary Because of the Children

Some battered women find it necessary to have regular or continuing contact with an abusive ex-partner because of child visitation rights or joint custody. Ex-partners often use these contacts, which are most often phone contacts, to verbally abuse their ex-wives. They may take these contacts as an opportunity to be accusatory, say cruel things, or try to make the woman feel small ("You're too needy . . . You're crazy . . . You're a bad mother"). Under such circumstances, we advise women to tell their ex-partners, "You have a relationship with the children, but you do not have a relationship with me. If you bring up anything other than something important about the children, I am going to say good-bye. Also, if you criticize me or put me down, I am going to say good-bye."

If calls are primarily for the purpose of speaking to the children, we advise women not to say anything beyond "hello" and then to immediately call to your child, saying "Your father's on the phone."

Role-Playing a Potential Conversation

If your anxiety is high when you face your ex-partner, your ability to function may be seriously impaired. For example, in states of high anxiety (and particularly if there is no plan of action), you may freeze up or act impulsively in ways that are negatively influential. It is therefore a good idea to practice what you might say in a real conversation.

In cognitive trauma therapy, we simulate interactions with a role-playing exercise. First, we simulate telephone interactions, and then we simulate face-to-face interactions. Initially, the therapist plays the role of the client, and the client plays the role of her ex-partner. The phone interaction starts with the therapist saying, "Ring, ring," picking up an imaginary phone, and saying, "Hello." Then the client says what she thinks her ex-partner might say, and the therapist responds in ways we've recommended above. After role-playing this way for a while, therapist and client switch roles, with the client playing herself and the therapist playing the role of the ex-partner. This exercise allows clients to practice what they are going to say if and when they have contacts with former partners, and usually results in lowering clients' anxiety about the prospect of contacts with ex-partners.

We recommend that you engage in this same exercise described above with a friend or relative.

What did you learn from this chapter and the role-playing exercise?

_____

_____

_____

_____

CHAPTER 14

Overcoming Fear by Exposure to Harmless Reminders

In chapter 7, you learned that all your efforts to avoid thoughts or memories of your abusive relationship have given you temporary relief, which has unwittingly or inadvertently contributed to the persistence of your PTSD. You also learned that one of the paths to recovery from your PTSD is to deliberately expose yourself to reminders of your abusive relationship.

In cognitive trauma therapy, when we suggest that clients deliberately expose themselves to reminders of their abuse or abuser as a homework exercise, they will occasionally respond, "Do I have to?" To which the therapist may respond, "I hope you never *have to* do anything again as long as you live. I only want you to engage in these exercises if you think it is a good idea and think it will help you recover from your PTSD." The same holds for you. In this chapter, we are going to suggest that you deliberately expose yourself to harmless reminders of your abuse and your abuser as a means of helping you get rid of your PTSD. However, we only want you to do what we suggest if you think it's a good idea and will benefit you in the long run.

In cognitive trauma therapy, we ask clients to complete a survey that lists eighteen types of potentially anxiety-evoking activities (such as watching movies or reading articles about domestic violence) that are not dangerous, but which many battered women avoid in order to preserve or obtain a state of relief. After they complete this survey, many of our clients are amazed at how many activities they routinely avoid, how constricted their lives have become, and how much energy it takes to be chronically avoidant. We want you to take your life back and become all that you can be. We believe that if you can find the courage to face reminders of pain from the past and do things you didn't think you could do, you will feel empowered and liberated, with enhanced self-esteem and peace of mind.

Exposing Yourself to Reminders of Your Abuse and Abuser

In *prolonged exposure*, the most widely employed exposure therapy, clients are asked to repeatedly reexperience or relive the trauma in visualizations until memories and images of the trauma no longer evoke anxiety or fear (Foa and Rothbaum 1998). Rather than doing prolonged exposure—in which you might visualize and dwell on specific incidents of abuse—we are going to recommend that you engage in four types of *indirect exposure* exercises, which may or may not trigger memories of abuse. We are going to ask you to

1. Look at pictures or photographs of your abusive ex-partner (if you have any) and to imagine yourself looking at him.

2. Expose yourself to smells, tastes, and songs that remind you of the abuse or your abuser.

3. Watch movies that portray domestic violence.

4. Engage in other activities or go to places that remind you of the abuse or your abuser.

Looking at Pictures of Your Ex-Partner and Visualizing Him

Do you have any pictures of your ex-partner? If you don't, we are not surprised. Many of our clients tore up such pictures or threw them away because they did not want to be reminded of their abuser and what he did to them. If you have pictures or have access to pictures of your former abuser, would you be willing to look at pictures of him for five minutes every day until you are no longer bothered by the exercise?   Yes ____ No ____

If you checked yes, please write "I will look at pictures of _____ daily for five minutes on line number 1 of the Escape and Avoidance Busting Exposure Agreement, which is at the end of this chapter (p. 181).

If you have lots of pictures of your ex-partner, we would like you to select some pictures that remind you of the best times with him and some pictures that remind you of the worst times. Looking at pictures that remind you of the best times is likely to make you feel sad but will help you grieve the loss of a marital dream or what you once had. Looking at pictures that remind you of the worst times is likely to evoke anxiety, which will gradually dissipate.

It's always a good idea to schedule this activity. What time each day will you be willing to look at your ex-partner's pictures? (Write the time on the line under line 1 on the exposure agreement.)

We usually ask clients to perform this exposure exercise in the bathroom, where there is always privacy. Unless there is a reason that the bathroom would not be a good place to do this exercise, please look at your ex-partner's pictures five minutes each day in the bathroom.

If Your Answer Is Still No

If you indicated that you are unwilling to look at pictures of your ex-partner, we would like to ask you a couple more questions. (Otherwise, you can move on to the next section.) Do you want your ex-partner to be able to continue to get a rise out of you or control how you feel? For example, if he were looking at you, would you want him to see you get upset just thinking about him?

If you run into your ex-partner on the street or at Wal-Mart, would you rather be calm and relaxed or anxious and panicky?

In all likelihood, you don't want to get upset and you would rather be relaxed—because if you are relaxed, you are much less likely to do something rash or impulsive. Remember also that nothing about your ex-partner's physical appearance is dangerous. It's just like Millie and the light (from chapters 7 and 8). If we showed Millie a picture of your ex-partner every time we shocked her, she wouldn't want to look at your ex-partner either. However, just as the light itself had no power to inflict pain on Millie, your ex-partner's physical appearance has no power to inflict pain on you. You may not want to look at pictures of your ex-partner because his face and physical appearance were associated with the mean and hurtful things he did. Our goal here is to neutralize everything about your partner that can't hurt you.

Would you reconsider your decision and agree to look at pictures of your ex-partner five minutes a day? Yes _____ No _____ . If you checked yes, that would be great. If yes, please write "I will look at pictures of _____ for five minutes a day" on line 1 of the exposure agreement and indicate when you will to do this exercise each day on the next line.

If you are still unwilling to look at your ex-partner, we respect your decision. You do not have to do anything that you choose not to do. Perhaps, you will reconsider at a later time. Perhaps not. You are the captain of your own ship, and we respect the direction in which you choose to go. As your advocate, we can only make recommendations regarding what we think is in your long-term best interest, but the final decision is up to you.

Visualizing Him

Are you good at visualizing things? For example, if we asked you to imagine yourself in the supermarket, would you be able to make it fairly real—almost as if you were there? The more real you can imagine something happening, the more effective visualization can be as a technique for overcoming your anxiety or fear of anything that is not dangerous.

Would you be willing to visualize looking at your ex-partner for five minutes a day, immediately after looking at his pictures for five minutes?   Yes _____ No _____ . (If you do not have any pictures of your ex-partner, would you be willing to visualize him ten minutes a day?   Yes _____ No _____ .) If you checked yes, good for you, and please write "I will visualize myself looking at _____ for five (or ten) minutes a day" on line 2 of the exposure agreement.

Enhancing Reality

The more sensory dimensions (smell, sound, sight, touch) that you can create in a simulated experience, the more effective the simulation will be for desensitizing or reducing your level of fear or anxiety when faced with the actual situation. For example, in training pilots to function at a high level during hazardous flying conditions, trainers utilize a flight simulator in which pilots "fly a plane" in a real cockpit, with realistic visual and auditory effects, with the so-called plane shaking like a real airplane would under hazardous flying conditions.

If the simulated plane "crashes," the pilot will walk out of the plane unharmed because the simulated reality wasn't dangerous. The same thing is true when you look at pictures of your ex-partner or visualize him.

If possible, we would like you to add some dimensions of sound and smell to your experience of looking at pictures and visualizing your ex-partner. Did your ex-partner wear any kind of cologne or aftershave lotion that reminds you of him?   Yes _____ No _____ . If you checked yes, would you be willing to buy a small bottle and smell the fragrance while looking at pictures and visualizing him?   Yes _____ No _____ . If you checked yes, please write, "I will smell the cologne he wore while I visualize and look at pictures of _____" on the next line of the exposure agreement.

Did your ex-partner drink beer or hard liquor, the smell of which reminds you of him or the abuse?   Yes _____ No _____ . If you checked yes, would you be willing to buy a bottle of beer or a bottle of the hard liquor he drank, pour it in a towel, and smell the alcohol while looking at pictures and visualizing your ex-partner? Yes _____ No _____ . If you checked yes, please write, "I will smell alcohol while visualizing and looking at pictures of _____" on the next line of the exposure agreement.

Is there any type of music or are there any particular songs that your ex-partner liked and that remind you of him?   Yes _____ No _____ . If yes, what type of music did he like or what songs did he like?

Would you be willing to listen to his favorite type of music or a song or songs that he liked while looking at his pictures and visualizing him? Yes ____ No ____ . If you checked yes, please write, "I will listen to songs that he liked" on the next line of the exposure agreement.

We congratulate you for having the courage to engage in these exercises, and now we would like to discuss ways you can regulate or control your level of tension and distress while performing these exercises.

How to Regulate Your Tension Level

We have postponed assigning the exposure exercises until this chapter because we wanted you to acquire skills for managing stress and treating yourself with respect, both of which you can use during the exposure exercises. Here are some techniques for regulating your tension level while visualizing your abuser and looking at his photos.

1. Be superaware of your level of tension, and if you notice increases in muscle tension in any part of your body, take a couple of long, slow, deep breaths, tense the affected muscles for five to ten seconds, and then concentrate on letting go of the tension.

2. Be very aware of the thoughts going through your mind and try very hard to avoid any negative self-talk.

3. Try to avoid using any value judgments or negatively evaluative words, or any editorializing about the meaning of your abuser's behavior or intentions. For example, if you interpret your abuser's gaze as "sinister" or "evil," characterize him as having a "serial killer mentality," refer to him as a "pig" or "monster," or ask yourself, "why?" you are just going to get yourself worked up into a fit of anger. Remember, emotionally charged words are psychological shocks that can recharge thoughts and memories of abuse and your abuser with negative energy.

If engaging in these (or any of the other) exposure exercises results in your recalling incidents of abuse you haven't thought about for a long time, do not be alarmed. Having such memories surface will give you the opportunity to take the charge out of them and the negative effects these memories may have had on you without your awareness.

In the unlikely event that you experience intense distress while engaging in the exposure exercises, you may wish to suspend doing them for the time being or contact a therapist who specializes in the treatment of stress for support. Most therapists who are members of the Association for the Advancement of Behavior Therapy (AABT) share our theoretical orientation, and AABT maintains a clinical directory and referral service. This service is offered to help the general public locate behavior therapists in their area. If you have access to the Internet, you can reach this directory at www.aabt.org. Alternatively, you may visit our Web site (www.healingthetrauma.com) or call AABT's central office at (212) 647-1890 for assistance in finding a behavior therapist.

In the highly unlikely event that your distress does not subside within a reasonable period of time after you stop doing the exposure exercises, you may wish to call a crisis hotline, call your therapist (if you have one), or call a friend for support.

How Long Should You Do This?

If you do these exercises diligently, on a daily basis, for three or four weeks, you will probably get to the point where it will not bother you much, if at all, to look at pictures of your ex-partner or to imagine yourself looking at him. And if you actually see him, you will probably be much less anxious than you would be now. Would you be willing to do these exercises for thirty days?   Yes _____ No _____ . If you checked yes, please write, "I will do these visualization exercises for thirty days (or until I am not bothered at all doing them)" on the next blank line of the exposure agreement.

Watching Movies that Portray Domestic Violence

In cognitive trauma therapy, we always ask our clients to watch at least two movies on domestic violence. We ask them to watch *Sleeping with the Enemy* and *Once Were Warriors*. Have you seen *Sleeping with the Enemy*? Julia Roberts plays the role of a battered woman married to a wealthy man who, beneath a facade of sophistication and charm, is cruel and vicious. Are you willing to rent and watch *Sleeping with the Enemy*?   Yes _____ No _____ . If you checked yes, please write, "I will rent and watch *Sleeping with the Enemy*" on the next blank line of the exposure agreement. Then, on the next line, write when you will rent this movie and when you will watch it.

Once Were Warriors is probably the most graphic movie on domestic violence ever produced. The movie is fiction but is very realistic in the way it portrays domestic violence in New Zealand among the native Maoris. Are you also willing to watch *Once Were Warriors*? Yes _____ No _____ . We hope you checked yes. If you did, please write, "I will rent and watch *Once Were Warriors*" on the next blank line of the exposure agreement, and on the next line, write when you will rent and watch this movie.

We need to tell you a little bit more about *Once Were Warriors* before you watch so you won't be surprised or caught off guard when you see a scene of children overhearing domestic violence or when you see other violent scenes. There is one scene in which the children are terrified, huddled together in their bedroom, as they hear their father berate and beat their mother. In a scene late in the movie, the teenage daughter is betrayed and raped by a favorite uncle, a trauma which has far-reaching and tragic consequences.

Guidelines for Watching These Movies

There are several guidelines we would like you to follow while watching *Sleeping with the Enemy* and *Once Were Warriors.*

1. When you watch each of these movies, keep in mind that these are only movies—not real life, and no one is getting hurt. The violence is only simulated. For example, in *Sleeping with the Enemy*, Julia Roberts did not get any bruises. The abuse isn't real.

2. It is important that you watch each movie to its completion. If you do not finish the movies, there is a chance you may be giving yourself relief reinforcement that will strengthen rather than weaken your PTSD avoidance symptoms. It is perfectly all right to take breaks from watching the whole movie at one time, as long as you return and watch it until the end. And when you do get to the end, pat yourself on the back and congratulate yourself for doing something that may have been difficult at first or something you didn't think you could do.

3. After you have watched each movie, go back and rewatch scenes that were distressing to watch, and keep watching these scenes until they no longer bother you.

4. Be very aware of how your body is reacting as you watch the movies, and if you notice increases in tension, take a couple of long, slow, deep breaths, tense the affected muscles for five to ten seconds, and then concentrate on letting go of the tension.

Our goal here is not for you to be able to enjoy these movies (although some women find them enjoyable, since both movies are well acted). Our goal is for you to be able to watch these movies without becoming unduly upset, thereby helping you get over your PTSD.

Identifying Important Similarities between the Batterers

In certain respects, the batterers in *Sleeping with the Enemy* and *Once Were Warriors* were very different. The batterer in *Sleeping with the Enemy* was wealthy and sophisticated, and he controlled and violated his wife in very manipulative and premeditated ways. By contrast, the batterer in *Once Were Warriors* was an uneducated alcoholic, extremely impulsive, and violent both in and out of the marriage. Now that we have pointed out the differences between these two men, we want you to figure out—after you have watched both of these movies—how these two men are similar or alike. In other words, what are the important similarities (there are at least two) between these two abusive men that override or transcend their differences? Please bookmark this page and come back to this place and answer this question *after* you have watched both movies. (Please don't look below the line for the answers; skip ahead to "Engaging in Activities That Remind You of the Abuse" on the next page.)

_____

_____

First, both of these guys were extremely selfish, egotistical, and self-centered. Second, neither had any empathy, compassion, or the slightest concern about the suffering of the woman they claimed to love. Certainly, they had absolutely no guilt. Third, both of these guys were deceitfully charming when they wanted to be. Wrapping this all up, both of these guys were full-on sociopaths and would meet diagnostic criteria for antisocial personality disorder (American Psychiatric Association 1994).

Engaging in Activities That Remind You of the Abuse

Many formerly battered women avoid a variety of activities and avoid going to a variety of places that remind them of the abuse or their abuser. Examples of activities our clients have avoided include exercise; watching sports on TV; reading articles on violence; watching the news or TV programs that depict violence; eating certain kinds of food; and wearing makeup, jewelry, or certain kinds of clothes. Examples of places our clients have avoided include beaches, parks, restaurants, and shopping centers.

Have you been avoiding any activities or places that would remind you of the abuse or your abuser?   Yes _____ No _____ . If you checked yes, what activities and/or places have you been avoiding?

_____

_____

_____

_____

Are you willing to engage in any of these activities or go to any of these places? Yes _____ No _____ . If you checked yes, please write what activities you agree to engage in and/or what places you agree to go on the next empty line(s) of the exposure agreement. Also indicate when you will engage in these activities and/or go to these places.

What Else Have You Been Avoiding?

Is there anything else that you have been avoiding because it would make you anxious or uncomfortable and is related to your experiences of abuse?   Yes _____ No _____ . If you checked yes, what have you been avoiding?

_____

Are you willing to do what you have been avoiding?   Yes _____ No _____ . If you checked yes, please write down what you agree to do on the exposure agreement and write down when you are going to do it.

Some Exposure Success Stories

In two studies evaluating the effectiveness of cognitive trauma therapy, 90 percent of the 108 women who completed therapy no longer had PTSD at their post-therapy assessments (Kubany et al. 2003; Kubany et al. 2004). The great majority of these women had successfully performed exposure exercises and were no longer avoiding reminders of their abuse or abusers. We will provide a few examples of these exposure success stories.

Janette's Story

Janette had been engaging in the exposure exercise of visualizing her abusive ex-boyfriend for a couple weeks. At her next therapy session, her therapist asked Janette how this exposure exercise was going, and Janette said, "I'm actually enjoying it." Surprised by Janette's response, her therapist asked for an explanation. Janette replied, "He really was quite good-looking, you know." Janette had completely severed the connection between her ex-boyfriend's physical appearance and the abuse he inflicted. She was able to appreciate her ex-boyfriend's good looks while keeping them separate from her memory of the type of person he was and what he did to her.

Gretchen's Story

Gretchen's abusive ex-husband was obsessed with Nazi memorabilia and loved Wagner's music, which Gretchen came to hate. Out of the relationship for ten years, she still hated Wagner's music. Listening to this music was one of Gretchen's exposure assignments. At her next therapy session, Gretchen said, "It really is beautiful music. I don't think I ever realized that before."

Fran's Story

Fran was haunted by memories of her deceased husband, who had abused her for many years. It came to light in therapy that Fran's husband had an identical twin brother, Walter, who was always very nice to her but whom she had not seen for a long time. Fran agreed with her therapist to visit Walter, who would definitely remind her of her husband. When Walter opened the door, Fran said that she "started shaking like a leaf. It was as if my husband had risen from the dead." After a pleasant meeting with Walter, she invited him (at her therapist's suggestion) for a barbecue at the beach, where Fran's husband had beaten her badly, a place that she had been avoiding. At her next therapy session, Fran said that she and Walter had a wonderful time at the beach and that she was no longer bothered by memories of her deceased husband. Her therapist then said in jest, "It would be great if all my clients had an abusive partner who was off the planet and had an identical twin who was a nice guy." Our exposure work would go much faster with a virtual reality exercise (Rothbaum and Hodges 1999).

Chapter Follow-Up

Write down the day and date that is exactly fourteen days from today: _____ .
Mark this date on your calendar and bookmark this page. Over the next two weeks, conduct exposure exercises, according to the exposure agreement you've made. Then, after two weeks, come back to this spot in the workbook and answer the following questions:

What have you learned from engaging in the exposure exercises?

_____

_____

_____

_____

What have you learned from this chapter?

_____

_____

_____

_____

Escape and Avoidance Busting Exposure Agreement

I agree to engage in the following exposure exercises to overcome anxieties and fears about abuse- or abuser-related reminders that are not dangerous.

1. I will _____

   When: _____

2. I will _____

   When: _____

3. I will _____

   When: _____

4. I will _____

   When: _____

5. I will _____

   When: _____

6. I will _____

   When: _____

7. I will _____

   When: _____

8. I will _____

   When: _____

9. I will _____

   When: _____

10. I will _____

   When: _____

CHAPTER 15

How to Identify
Potential Perpetrators

Many formerly battered women are still attracted to men but may be reluctant to become involved in another romantic relationship because they aren't confident they will be able to identify someone who is likely to become abusive until it is too late. In this chapter you will learn how to identify potentially abusive men long before you become emotionally involved or have invested in a romantic relationship. If you know how to identify someone with abuse potential, it is likely that you will be less wary of men, be more comfortable spending time with men, and be more open to entertaining the possibility of getting romantically involved again at some point.

Red Flags That Someone Has the Potential to Be Abusive

We have identified twenty red flags, or early signs, that someone has the potential to become an abusive intimate partner. Each of these signs is described and discussed below.

    1. *Possessiveness.* A potentially abusive or predatory man tends to be very possessive or overcontrolling, sometimes causing his female partner to feel like he owns her. He may want to keep you all to himself and be overcontrolling about how and where

you spend your time. He may want to do everything with just the two of you. He may want you to quit other activities that you do without him. He may even want you to reduce the amount of time you spend with your family or close friends.

Another form of possessiveness would be his insistence that you account for all your time or whereabouts, frequently checking in to be sure you are "where you're supposed to be."

Sometimes, possessiveness is initially perceived by women as flattery. For example, getting several phone calls a day may be interpreted as strong attraction ("Gee, he really likes me"). What is something negative that repeated phone calls, even if the calls are made "lovingly," might signify?

Obsessive checking borders on stalking. By calling you repeatedly (or by persuading you to repeatedly call him), the man would be keeping track of your activities or where you are, and he might want to know where you were if he couldn't reach you. In the "loving," early stages of a relationship, he might say something like, "Gee, honey, I called you at three o'clock and couldn't reach you. I missed you. Where were you?"

2. *Jealousy.* Jealousy is a huge red flag. If a potential boyfriend is even slightly jealous, go the other way. Jealous men are insecure, tend to be very possessive and controlling, and are at high risk for becoming abusive.

3. *Dislike of your family or friends.* Does he find fault with or otherwise bad-mouth your friends or family? If he does, it does not bode well. Dislike of family or friends often results in a woman seeing less and less of them and sometimes even cutting ties completely. In fact, this sign and the two other warning signs we have identified thus far—possessiveness and jealousy—result in a woman becoming more and more socially isolated and vulnerable to abuse.

4. *In a hurry to get romantically involved.* Abusive men typically try to sweep women off their feet and rush them into romantic relationships. Similarly, abusive men will often try early on to get commitments from women to not go out with anyone else but them. They rush women into sexual relationships, rush women into moving in with them, and rush women into marriage. One woman who went through our program had four abusive husbands, and she married every one of them within two months of having met them.

Rushing a woman into a relationship is akin to stalking or obsessively checking up on you because, if a guy is spending a great deal of time with a woman, he always knows where she is and knows she cannot be spending time with other men.

5. *Lying.* Lying is another huge red flag. If you catch him in even the smallest lie, drop him like a hot potato. Predatory men are pathological liars and even lie when there is no reason to lie. For example, consider the following interaction:

Woman: Why did you say you weren't at the shopping mall yesterday?

Man: Because I wasn't there.

Woman: My sister saw you there!

Man: Your sister is nuts.

6. *Secretiveness.* Is he secretive about his activities or whereabouts? Are there large gaps of his time that you can't account for? And are there certain things he doesn't want to talk about, such as his prior intimate relationships? Does he talk on the phone with people who remain anonymous? Sometimes this can signify that he is involved in some illegal activity, such as using or dealing drugs. Some women do not find out until well into a relationship with an abusive man that he was using drugs or was a drug dealer.

7. *Imposition of his opinions or beliefs.* Does he try to impose his opinions or worldviews on you? Abusive men are opinionated, often with traditional sex-role beliefs favoring the dominance and authority of men in relationships with women.

8. *Belittling of your opinions or beliefs.* Does he belittle your opinions in even subtle ways, for example, saying things like, "You are so naive. Where have you been for the last twenty years? You really don't know what you're talking about."

9. *A bad temper.* Many abusive men are explosive. Does he have a bad temper—even if most of the time he seems to be so happy-go-lucky or mellow?

10. *Physical aggressiveness with someone else.* Have you seen him—or heard stories of him— being physically aggressive with someone else? Abusive men who are violent outside the relationship as well as with their girlfriends or wives are as a group the most maritally violent (Holtzworth-Munroe and Stuart 1994).

11. *Verbal mistreatment of other people.* If a potential boyfriend is being nice to you, but you see or hear him being verbally abusive to someone else, such as an employee or relative, this is a cause for concern.

12. *Blames others for his problems or mistakes.* Abusive men tend to blame others—the boss, you—for their own mistakes or problems of their own making. If something goes wrong, it's always somebody else's fault.

13. *"Playful" use of force during sex.* Some abusive men get unduly rough during sex in the name of "fun." Does he throw you down? Does he hold you down against your will during sex?

14. *A regular or past heavy user of alcohol or drugs.* Many men with histories of heavy alcohol or drug abuse are sociopathic (Morgenstern et al. 1997), with inclinations to become abusive with their intimate partners. In two studies at a residential substance abuse program, 90 percent of the women residents had been physically

hurt by an intimate partner, and almost all of them had been abused by a partner who had a problem with alcohol or drugs (Tremayne and Kubany 1998). About the only place that is more risky for meeting a batterer than a bar is an Alcoholics Anonymous or Narcotics Anonymous meeting.

15. *Reputation as a womanizer.* If a potential boyfriend has a reputation as a womanizer or if you know he has cheated on someone in the past, be very wary. Also, if he has been previously married, ask him if he wore a wedding ring. Many abusive men do not wear wedding rings because they do not want women they flirt and try to get sexually involved with to know that they are married.

16. *Unreliability.* Many abusive men are irresponsible and extraordinarily unreliable. Does he call you when he says he's going to call you? Does he pick you up when he says he's going to pick you up? Does he do what he says he is going to do when he says he is going to do it?

17. *Acts differently when you are alone than when you are with others.* What if a guy is sweet and loving toward you when the two of you are alone but is somewhat aloof or stand-offish when you are with other people, especially your girlfriends or other women? What might this behavior pattern signify?

He may not want other women to know that he is taken. If other women know he is going with or seriously involved with you, they will become upset and offended if he starts hitting on them. We had a battered woman client whose husband's circle of acquaintances did not even know that she and her husband were married.

18. *Invasion of your privacy.* Many abusive men have no qualms about invading the privacy of their girlfriends and wives, and they may even accuse their girlfriends and wives of "making a big deal over nothing" when they do. Does he open your mail or your e-mail? Does he check your phone messages? Does he look through your purse? Does he go through your closet or look through your dresser drawers?

19. *Cruelty to animals or children.* Does he mistreat animals? It has been estimated that approximately half of male batterers mistreat or even torture family pets (Ascione 2000). Does he expect children to do things that are far beyond their ability to do? Does he tease a child until he or she cries?

20. *Charm or charisma.* Many predatory men can be extraordinarily charming, witty, and fun to be with. They can also appear to be very empathic or understanding about a woman's reports of problems in her past, and some can even cry on demand. Charm or charisma is by no means a certain sign that a guy is going to become abusive, but abusive men as a group are probably far more charming than men who are not going to abuse their girlfriends or wives. We suspect that one of the reasons many abusive men are capable of being so charming is that they may have

no trouble giving women compliments that are exaggerations or lies. Be suspicious if a man is extremely complimentary—for example, if he tells you how absolutely wonderful you are before he really knows you.

Signs Exhibited by Your Abusive Partner before He Abused You

Below, place checkmarks next to the red flags, or warning signs, exhibited by your abusive partner before he became abusive with you.

_____ possessiveness

_____ jealousy

_____ dislike of your family or friends

_____ in a hurry to get romantically involved

_____ lying

_____ secretiveness

_____ imposition of his opinions or beliefs

_____ belittling of your opinions or beliefs

_____ a bad temper

_____ physical aggressiveness with someone else

_____ verbal mistreatment of other people

_____ blames others for his problems or mistakes

_____ "playful" use of force during sex

_____ a regular or past heavy use of alcohol or drugs

_____ reputation as a womanizer

_____ unreliability

_____ acts differently when you are alone than when you are with others

_____ invasion of your privacy

_____ cruelty to animals or children

_____ charm or charisma

Would you have gotten intimate or emotionally involved with him if you were aware that these were warning signs beforehand?

Identifying the Potential Abuser Early On

Many formerly battered women are particularly anxious early on in a new relationship, before they know a man very well and when he is being "such a nice guy," because they are uncertain of their ability to tell if he could be abusive. For example, many of our clients have said things like, "My husband was also a really nice guy when I first met him. And look what he turned out to be." To help you with this concern, we are now going to teach you what you can proactively do early in a relationship to tell whether a guy is a potential abuser.

Sociopathic, controlling men—who are likely to become abusive—have a communication skill deficit and have no interest whatsoever in learning how to improve in this area. It will be important for you to identify this skill deficit so that you can break off a relationship with a guy before you get emotionally involved. This deficit is often manifested or exhibited during marriage counseling that isn't working. It is the most common problem in dysfunctional marriages. It is a communication skill deficit that manifests itself when there is conflict. Can you think of what this skill deficit might be?

Abusive men are selfish and controlling and want to force their will on their girlfriends and wives. The communication skill deficit we are talking about is the inability and lack of desire to resolve conflict in a mutually respectful way. Abusive men cannot, and have no interest in learning how to, resolve conflict in a mutually respectful way. Abusive men can be extremely charming and fool many people when things are going well. However, they are very self-centered and controlling and will react negatively when others will not let them have their way. Provoking conflict with abusive men will trigger or activate their tendencies to become overcontrolling and verbally abusive. Their true colors are very likely to show when there is conflict. When there is conflict, abusive men exhibit a strong tendency to become verbally aggressive and controlling.

Now that you know what this deficit is, you need to figure out a way to determine whether a potential boyfriend has this problem. How can you find out whether a guy is unable and unwilling to resolve conflict in a mutually respectful way?

Although it may surprise you to hear this, you need to provoke conflict. As one of our clients said, "Yeah. Piss him off!"

Provoking conflict is the last thing that would occur to most of our clients when they first start therapy. They were habitually conflict avoidant because conflict reminded them of their previous abuse. Also, when they were in an abusive relationship, it was dangerous to get mad or disagree because when they did talk back or stand up for their rights, the abuse got worse.

Provoking Conflict Early in a Relationship Is Not Dangerous

It is important for you to know that it is not dangerous to provoke conflict early in a relationship because an abusive man knows that a woman will not go out with him anymore if he becomes physically or even verbally abusive before she is emotionally involved or invested in the relationship. Most women do not become emotionally invested or committed to make a relationship work before there is sexual intimacy—at the earliest—or until she has become pregnant, has moved in with a guy, or has married him. Abusive men rarely abuse women before they have had sex (at the earliest), or until she is pregnant, or until after she moves in with him, or on or soon after their wedding day. You would be surprised how many battered women are first abused on their wedding day or shortly thereafter. When did your abusive partner first abuse you?

Ways of Provoking Conflict

Again, provoking conflict early in the relationship will tell you a lot about how this man handles conflict. If he handles it well, you can be more confident that he has the potential to be a good partner. Here are a few ideas.

Disagree and Be "Selfish"

Disagree and be "selfish" early on in the relationship. Argue your viewpoints when they differ from his and disagree when you do disagree. Disagree about politics, sports, TV program preferences, anything where your opinions are different from his. Insist on getting your wants met in the relationship as well as on engaging in activities you enjoy as well as those he enjoys. Do not be so nice that you are willing to do anything he wants to do. For example, you might say, "We've gone to two movies that you like and haven't gone to a movie that I like. This Sunday, I would like us to go to a movie that I like." If you say something like this on the second or third date, and he says something like, "What are you, a feminist?" you can say, "Nice knowing you."

Many formerly battered women find it foreign to "make a fuss over little things." But that is exactly what we suggest you do. One of our clients said she didn't have a single argument with her abusive boyfriend until the day he hit her and broke her jaw. Her therapist probed for examples of earlier conflict. The woman recalled that she didn't like his cologne, so she bought him another kind, but he wouldn't wear it. She said that she didn't pursue the issue because she didn't want to jeopardize the relationship "over such a little thing." To which her therapist responded, "You mean his cologne means more to him than you do? You're darned right you make a fuss about such a little thing! Find out what kind of guy he is."

In chapter 12, we gave you an example of a woman who made a big deal about her boyfriend's objection to their ordering a pizza with all the pepperoni (which she did not like) on one side of the pizza. He wanted her to pick the pepperoni off of her pieces. She provoked conflict by telling him she wanted to go home if they didn't order pizza with the pepperoni on one side.

If you have children, you may wish to insist that every other time you get together that it be a family affair. Many abusive men won't like this because they would prefer getting together with just the two of you.

One of our clients narrowly avoided getting involved with an abuser as a result of inadvertently and unintentionally provoking conflict on their second date. They were driving to a restaurant when he saw something out of the corner of his eye and said, "Don't turn around." What do you think she did? Right. She turned around. In response, the guy verbally "went off on her," hurling obscenities and insults. When they got to the restaurant, our client asked him to take her home, and she never went out with him again. (This example also illustrates why abusive men self-consciously try not to be abusive before a woman is emotionally involved; they know she will stop seeing him if he acts this way before she really cares about him.)

Some potential abusers who perceive you are the type of woman who wants equality out of a relationship won't even call back for a second date. In response to this comment, one of our clients said, "I guess that's a compliment."

Postpone Sexual Intimacy and Issue an Ultimatum on the Discussion of Sex

On your first date with a guy, we suggest that you tell him up front that you have zero tolerance for abuse. For example, you might say something like, "I have no idea whether you and I have any future together, but I want to tell you something. I have been in an abusive relationship, and I want you to know that I will *never* be in an abusive relationship again. I don't want to get into details about what happened. However, if you ever think about getting physically abusive with me, I want you to know that if you do, the first time will be the last time. I will end the relationship right then and there. I also want you to know that if you ever start verbally abusing me—for example, swearing at me or calling me dirty names— you will be inviting me to call it quits."

We recommend that you also tell him you are planning to postpone sexual intimacy. For example, you might say, "I have been stung in the past, so I am not going to get intimate with anyone until I know them really, really well. I just want to tell you that up front so that you won't have any false expectations."

And if he then asks, "How long is that going to take?" tell him something like, "I don't have any idea." If he is only interested in sex, your decision not to have sex will be a nice indirect way to provoke conflict. If the person generally enjoys your company, he'll stick around and not keep pressuring you for sex.

If a guy pressures you for sex, tell him you want him to stop bringing up sex, and that "if and when I'm ready for sex, I'll let you know." If he persists, tell him that if he won't change the subject you are going to end the conversation and go home. Then, if he brings up the subject again, end the conversation and go home. Also tell him that you will not continue dating someone who continues to pressure you for sex. You might say, "If you want to continue dating me, you are going to have to stop talking about sex." If he keeps bringing up sex, we suggest that you terminate the relationship.

Do Not Be Rushed into a Relationship

Go slow. We recommend that for the first several months of a relationship you be unwilling to get together more than once a week. Do not allow him to rush you or pressure you to get together more frequently. Abusive men are impatient and will probably break off the relationship if a woman sticks to her guns and only gets together once a week or less and without sex.

Tell Him You Are Going to Continue Dating Other People

Tell a guy when you start going out with him that you are going to continue to date other people and will never date only one person until you are in love and have been intimate. Also, after you have gone out for a while, we recommend that you program in a date or night out with someone else (even if it is just a male friend whom you have no romantic interest in).

Insist on Reliability

On the first or second date, we recommend that you tell a potential boyfriend that his reliability is important to you. For example, you might say, "Do you want to know what I'm looking for in a guy? I'm looking for a guy I can count on—someone who is reliable. I am looking for someone who calls me when he says he is going to call me. Someone who picks me up when he says he is going to pick me up. Someone who does what he says he is going to do when he says he is going to do it."

Then, if he doesn't follow through on something, remind him of what you are looking for. Then, you might tell him, "I will not continue to go out with someone I can't count on," and perhaps postpone your next date for at least a week. For example, you might say, "I can't make it next Saturday. How about a week from Saturday?"

Program in an Unexplained Refusal to Get Together

Even after you are going out with a guy on a regular basis, program in a refusal to get together. For example, if he asks you out next week, tell him, "I can't make it next week" (without an explanation). How about the following week?" If he asks you why you can't make it, repeat that you can't make it. If he continues to pressure you for a reason, tell him you want to change the subject. If he still persists, ask him if he wants to go out with you in two weeks, because if he continues to ask why you can't go out with him next week, you are not going to go out with him in two weeks.

Find Out about His Prior Relationships

What is something you want to know about him? You're probably curious about his previous relationships. For example:

- How many girlfriends (and wives) has he had?

- What did they argue or disagree about?

- How did they resolve their differences?

- What differences didn't they resolve?

- Why did they break up?

Abusive men will be threatened by this line of questioning and may go on the offensive. For example, they may get angry or accuse you of being insecure. To which you might say, "That's not a nice thing to say," or "You don't have to tell me, but if you don't tell me, I am not going to go out with you again." Then, he may accuse you of being a hypocrite because you won't tell him about your abuse history. If he does this, say that these are two different subjects. If he doesn't want to date you anymore because you're not willing to talk about your past, that is his right and his choice. You are simply telling him the conditions under which you would be willing to continue to see him.

Check Out His Background

In the workplace, employers check out job applicants' references before they make important hiring decisions. It's just good business. Certainly, making a romantic commitment to man has greater implications for a woman's well-being than hiring a key employee for her business. For example, you can always fire an employee if he doesn't work out. It's much more complicated getting out of a bad marriage. Therefore, if you get to the point that you are considering having sexual intercourse with a guy, or are considering moving in with him or accepting his proposal of marriage, we recommend that you check out his background. We recommend that you tell your boyfriend that you want to speak personally to his ex-girlfriend(s) or ex-wife and ask for their phone numbers. If he gets upset, tell him something like, "This doesn't have anything to do with you. I intended to do this before we ever met. If you don't have anything to hide, you don't have anything to worry about." If the guy breaks off the relationship over this issue, you can be certain he has something to hide.

In some states, it is possible to do a search of a person's criminal record. If a boyfriend has a criminal record that you didn't know about, he is a bad bet for a good relationship.

How Do You Feel Now?

Are you more confident now than you were before you read this chapter that you have the skill or ability to identify a guy with abuse potential?

What did you learn from reading this chapter and answering the questions?

_____

_____

_____

_____

CHAPTER 16

Self-Advocacy Review: How Have You Changed?

In chapter 2, we discussed problem areas in five interrelated styles of functioning, all of which reflect a lack of self-advocacy. These styles of functioning include:

- placing other people's wants ahead of your own

- unassertiveness and tolerance of disrespect

- decision making driven by "supposed tos"

- inability to deal with hostility

- negative self-talk

You probably weren't a very strong advocate for yourself when you first picked up this book. In fact, all of these styles of functioning characterized almost all of our battered women clients when they started cognitive trauma therapy. Unfortunately, many women—not just formerly battered women—are not very strong advocates for themselves. In the United States and throughout the world, women have been socialized to be and to believe they are subordinate to men and need to do the bidding of men in a male-dominated world.

In chapter 2, we also introduced you to twenty-five self-advocacy strategies that can enable you to empower yourself by taking control of your life and taking charge of your own future happiness. We asked you to write what you believed about each strategy and how important or relevant it was for you. We asked you to complete this self-advocacy exercise early in the workbook because we believed the experience might give you a road map of what you wanted to accomplish through this workbook. Our self-advocacy strategies can be summed up by the following five styles of functioning, all of which reflect self-advocacy and are important keys to any woman's future happiness:

- putting yourself first and placing a high priority on getting your own wants and needs satisfied

- assertiveness and intolerance of disrespect

- decision making driven by self-assessments of what is in your best interest

- ability to deal with negative or disrespectful comments

- talking to yourself (in speech and thought) with the same respect that you deserve to get from others

Most of the chapters after chapter 2 were designed in one way or another to educate you about the importance of these styles of functioning and to put these strategies into practice in ways that you think and in ways that you behave.

Now we are going ask you to repeat the original exercise, to give yourself the opportunity to see just how far you have come as a result of completing this workbook. We would like you to reassess your attitudes about self-advocacy by responding to the same twenty-five self-advocacy strategies that you responded to in chapter 2.

Self-Advocacy Strategies Questionnaire

Instructions: To recover fully from the effects of trauma, you need to become your own strongest advocate. Listed below are twenty-five self-advocacy strategies that will help you to promote your best interests and empower yourself. If you adopt or embrace and come to live by these statements, your recovery from trauma will go forward at a rapid pace.

First, read through the entire questionnaire. Then, read each statement again and write down what this statement means to you. Is it true for you? If not, do you want it to be true? How does or could this self-advocacy strategy help you?

Today's Date: _____

1. "Getting my wants and needs satisfied is more important than satisfying the needs of someone else. I need to make my best interests and wants a top priority. (Advocating for my best interest means to do things and make decisions that promote the long-term happiness and quality of life for me and my children.)" What do you believe about these statements and how they are relevant for you?

_____

2. "Getting my wants and needs satisfied belongs at the top of my daily to do list. If I don't put myself first, who will? If I get my needs satisfied, I will have more energy to satisfy the wants and needs of others." What do you believe about these statements and how they are relevant for you?

---

3. "It does not promote my long-term happiness to think or talk about things that I cannot change—such as dwelling on the unfairness of the system or past injustices. The time I spend on such things is time I cannot spend working on things I can control, change, or do something about. Time spent doing things of little value costs me the opportunity of spending that time doing something that is more worthwhile. In other words, spending time on things I can't change does not belong on my daily to do list!"

---

4. "To get my needs met, I need to tell people how I feel and what I want. Other people cannot read my mind and won't know how I feel or what I want unless I tell them."

---

5. "I need to stand up for my rights and not allow myself to be taken advantage of. I not only deserve respect I must demand respect. (To demand respect means to not tolerate disrespect.)"

---

6. "I need to make decisions based on what is in my best interest (and my children's best interest). I need to stop doing things because I think I should. (The question to ask myself when trying to decide what to do is 'What course of action is most likely to promote my long-term happiness or quality of life?')"

---

7. "When I do something or make a decision in order to get immediate relief from painful feelings, chances are good that I am not acting in my best interest."

---

8. "If a decision will lead to either guilt or resentment, go with guilt! Because it is more likely I will be acting in my best interest rather than someone else's."

_____

_____

9. "Strong feelings associated with thoughts or ideas are not evidence that these ideas are correct (or incorrect). It is not in my best interest to make important decisions based on how I feel about things; important decisions should be made on the basis of the evidence and an intellectual analysis of what is in my best interest."

_____

_____

10. "Am I in a high state of distress (anxiety, worry, dread, depression) about an important decision I 'should' or 'have to' make? Any course of action that will give me immediate relief from this distress is not likely to be in my best interest. I need to achieve a state of calm before making any important decision. Otherwise, I may make an impulsive decision that is bad for me in the long run. I will be more objective and think more clearly if I am calm when I select my course of action."

_____

_____

11. "Just because somebody says that I have negative qualities does not mean it's true. However, I do not have control over the words that come out of other people's mouths. I just need to remember that words are just sound waves (not fists or baseball bats)."

_____

_____

12. "Just because someone blames me (or blamed me) does not mean it was my fault."

_____

_____

13. "Just because someone apologizes to me for some wrongdoing does not mean I am now obligated to do what that person wants or go back to the way things were (whether or not I forgive the person)."

_____

_____

14. "If I never say 'could have' or 'should have' again, I will be a happier person."

_____

_____

15. "Tearing myself down ('I'm worthless . . . I'm stupid . . . I'm never going to be happy,' etc.) makes me depressed and want to give up or go away. I need to start treating myself with the same respect that I would like to get—and deserve—from others."

_____

_____

16. "When talking about things I don't like about myself, it's much better to say 'this is the way I have been (or have done things) in the past' rather than 'this is the way I am or what I always do.' The latter implies that this is the way I am always going to be; the former implies that I can do things differently in the future."

_____

_____

17. "Just because I think a thought or have an idea does not mean the thought or idea is true. I need to stop automatically believing everything that comes into my mind. The thoughts may just be bad habits. I need to evaluate the evidence for some of the irrational ideas that pop into my mind."

_____

_____

18. "I need to stop saying 'I feel' this or that way with words that are not emotions (for example, 'I feel stuck, obligated, overwhelmed'). Instead, I need to examine the evidence for thinking that I am stuck, obligated, or overwhelmed. If I evaluate the evidence for these negative ideas, I may realize I'm not really stuck, obligated, overwhelmed, and so on."

_____

_____

19. "I need to stop asking 'why?' Knowing why will not change what happened, and it keeps me stuck in the past."

_____

_____

20. "I may have been helpless and out of control when I was abused by my partner or when I was a child; but I am not powerless or out of control now."

_____

_____

21. "If I focus on possible solutions to my problems, I may solve them. If I focus on reasons why my problems can't be solved, my problems will be solved only if I get lucky."

_____

_____

22. "I am an innocent survivor and am likable and lovable. I also deserve to be happy."

_____

_____

23. "When a woman says, 'I feel sorry for him,' she is making the other person's problem her problem. If I feel sorry for him, I'm supposed to do something about it. I should do something that he would like me to do (go back to him; stay in the relationship). This is faulty thinking! I may not like to see him suffer, but it may be contrary to my best interest to do something that reduces my guilt and alleviates his 'pain.' I am not responsible for solving the problems that he caused and for which he needs to be held accountable. (Otherwise, he'll never learn and will continue to treat other women the way he treated me.) If I do something that he wants because I feel sorry for him, it means that I may be placing his wants and interests above my own (and my children's) best interest. I must act in my best interest."

_____

_____

24. "When someone says, 'I had to,' it usually means she chose to. Ordinarily, only children, slaves, prisoners, and people threatened with violence have to comply. In most cases, when we do something that somebody expects us to do, even when we don't want to do it, we choose to do it. I am not going to get physically hurt if I do not comply with a request or demand! I can choose to say no. This distinction is important because when I have choices, I have power and am in control. When I perceive myself as not having choices ('I had to'), I am powerless and out of control. For example, when I say someone is 'taking advantage of me,' it usually means that I am allowing that person to take advantage. This latter phrase implies that I can do something to stop unfair treatment and prevent it from happening in the future."

_____

_____

25. "When I get out of bed tomorrow, who is going to decide whether or not I am going to have a good day? Me or someone else? Of course, I want to be the one who decides. However, if I'm hoping that someone doesn't ruin my day by treating me in a certain way, I am going to have a good day only if I get lucky, like being in a rudderless boat praying that a friendly wind will blow me ashore rather than out to sea. On the other hand, if I know I am going to have a good day, no matter what (or in spite of what) someone else says or does, I am in control of my well-being."

_____

_____

How Have You Changed?

Now, we would like you to compare what you wrote about each of these statements today with what you wrote about each of them in chapter 2. After you have finished comparing what you wrote today with what you wrote earlier, come back to this place in the workbook and answer this question: How have you changed?

_____

_____

_____

_____

_____

_____

If you are like most of the women who have completed cognitive trauma therapy, you may be pleasantly surprised to find that your attitudes have changed considerably, even drastically. You may have even changed to the point where you seem like a different person—a proud woman who has become vastly empowered. Congratulations!

References

American Psychiatric Association. 1994. *Diagnostic and Statistical Manual of Mental Disorders.* 4th ed. Washington, D.C.: American Psychiatric Association.

Ascione, F. R. 2000. *Safe Haven for Pets: Guidelines for Programs Sheltering Pets for Women Who Are Battered.* Logan, Utah: Author.

Baer, J. 1976. *How to Be an Assertive (Not Aggressive) Woman in Life, in Love, and on the Job: A Total Guide to Self-Assertiveness.* New York: New American Library.

Berkowitz, L. 1973. Words and symbols as stimuli to aggressive responses. In *Control of Aggression: Implications for Basic Research.* Edited by J. F. Knutson. Chicago, Ill.: Aldine-Atherton.

Bureau of Justice Statistics. 1995. *Violence against Women: Estimates from the Redesigned Survey.* Washington, D.C.: Bureau of Justice.

Fischhoff, B. 1975. Hindsight does not equal foresight: The effect of outcome knowledge on judgment under uncertainty. *Journal of Experimental Psychology: Human Perception and Performance* 1:288–299.

Foa, E. B., D. S. Riggs, and E. Massie. 1995. The impact of fear activation and anger on the efficacy of exposure treatment for post-traumatic stress disorder. *Behavior Therapy* 26:487–499.

Foa, E. B., and B. O. Rothbaum. 1998. *Treating the Trauma of Rape.* New York: Guilford Press.

Frederiksen, L. W. 1975. Treatment of ruminative thinking by self-monitoring. *Journal of Behavior Therapy and Experimental Psychiatry* 6:258–259.

Friedman, H. S. 1992. *Hostility, Coping, and Health.* Washington, D.C.: American Psychological Association.

Golding, J. 1994. Sexual assault history and physical health in randomly selected Los Angeles women. *Health Psychology* 13:130–138.

Holtzworth-Munroe, A., and G. L. Stuart. 1994. Typologies of male batterers: Three subtypes and the differences among them. *Psychological Bulletin* 116:476–497.

Jacobson, N. S., J. M. Gottman, J. Waltz, R. Rushe, J. Babcock, and A. Holtzworth-Monroe. 1994. Affect, verbal content, and psychophysiology in the arguments of couples with a violent husband. *Journal of Consulting and Clinical Psychology* 62:982–988.

Jakubowski, P., and A. J. Lang. 1978. *The Assertive Option: Your Rights and Responsibilities.* Champaign, Ill.: Research Press.

Jehu, D. 1989. Mood disturbances among women clients sexually abused in childhood: Prevalence, etiology, treatment. *Journal of Interpersonal Violence* 4:164–184.

Korotitsch, W. J., and R. O. Nelson-Gray. 1999. An overview of self-monitoring research in assessment and treatment. *Psychological Assessment* 11:415–425.

Kubany, E. S. 1995, March. Social impact of five different kinds of "I" messages. Poster presented at the 75th Annual Western Psychological Association Convention, Los Angeles.

Kubany, E. S. 2000. Cross-validation of the trauma-related guilt inventory. Poster presented at the sixteenth annual meeting of the International Society for Traumatic Stress Studies. San Antonio, Texas.

Kubany, E. S., F. R. Abueg, J. M. Brennan, J. A. Owens, A. Kaplan, and S. Watson. 1995a. Initial examination of a multidimensional model of trauma-related guilt: Applications to combat veterans and battered women. *Journal of Psychopathology and Behavioral Assessment* 17:353–376.

Kubany, E. S., G. B. Bauer, D. C. Richard, and M. Y. Muraoka. 1995b. Impact of labeled anger and blame in intimate relationships. *Journal of Social and Clinical Psychology* 14:53–60.

Kubany, E. S., S. N. Haynes, F. R. Abueg, F. P. Manke, J. M. Brennan, and C. Stahura. 1996. Development and validation of the trauma-related guilt inventory (TRGI). *Psychological Assessment* 8:428–444.

Kubany, E. S., E. E. Hill, and J. A. Owens. 2003. Cognitive trauma therapy for formerly battered women with PTSD: Preliminary findings. *Journal of Traumatic Stress* 16:81–91.

Kubany, E. S., E. E. Hill, J. A. Owens, C. Iannce-Spencer, M. A. McCaig, K. Tremayne, and P. Williams. 2004. Cognitive trauma therapy for battered women with PTSD (CTT-BW). *Journal of Consulting and Clinical Psychology* 72:3–18.

Kubany, E. S., M. B. Leisen, A. S. Kaplan, and M. P. Kelly. 2000. Validation of a brief measure of post-traumatic stress disorder: The distressing event questionnaire (DEQ). *Psychological Assessment* 12:192–209.

Kubany, E. S., and F. P. Manke. 1995. Cognitive therapy for trauma-related guilt (CT-TRG): Conceptual bases and treatment outlines. *Cognitive and Behavioral Practice* 2:23–61.

Kubany, E. S., D. C. Richard, and G. B. Bauer. 1992. Impact of assertive and aggressive communication of distress and anger: A verbal component analysis. *Aggressive Behavior* 18:337–348.

Kubany, E. S., G. Tice, M. A. McCaig, J. R. Laconsay, and T. C. Ralston. 2003. Antisocial characteristics of men who batter women and men who don't. Poster presented at the 75th Annual Western Psychological Association Convention in Honolulu, HI. Manuscript submitted for publication.

Kubany, E. S., and S. B. Watson. 2003. Guilt: Elaboration of a testable multidimensional model. *The Psychological Record* 53:51–90.

Kulka, R. A., W. E. Schlenger, J. A. Fairbank, R. L. Hough, B. K. Jordan, C. R. Marmar, and D. S. Weiss. 1990. *Trauma and the Vietnam war generation: Report of the findings from the National Veterans Readjustment Study*. New York: Brunner/Mazel.

Leith, K. P., and R. F. Baumeister. 1996. Why do bad moods increase self-defeating behavior? Emotion, risk taking, and self-regulation. *Journal of Personality and Social Psychology* 71:1250–1267.

Morgenstern, J., J. Langenbucher, E. Labouvie, and K. J. Miller. 1997. The comorbidity of alcoholism and personality in a clinical population: Prevalence rates and relation to alcohol typology behaviors. *Journal of Abnormal Psychology* 106:74–84.

Muraoka, M. Y., J. G. Carlson, and C. M. Chemtob. 1998. Twenty-four-hour ambulatory blood pressure and heart rate monitoring in combat-related post-traumatic stress disorder. *Journal of Traumatic Stress* 11:473–484.

Ozer, E. M., and A. Bandura. 1990. Mechanisms governing empowerment effects: A self-efficacy analysis. *Journal of Personality and Social Psychology* 58:472–486.

Pitman, R. K., B. Altman, E. Greenwald, R. E. Longpre, M. L. Macklin, R. E. Poire', and G. S. Steketee. 1991. Psychiatric complications during flooding therapy for posttraumatic stress disorder. *Journal of Clinical Psychiatry* 52:17–20.

Resick, P. A., P. Nishith, T. L. Weaver, M. C. Astin, and C. A. Feuer. 2002. A comparison of cognitive processing therapy with prolonged exposure for the treatment of post-traumatic stress disorder in female rape victims. *Journal of Consulting and Clinical Psychology* 70:867–879.

Rosen, L. N., and L. Martin. 2000. Personality characteristics that increase vulnerability to sexual harassment among U.S. Army soldiers. *Military Medicine* 165:709–713.

Rosenhan, D. L., and M. E. P. Seligman. 1989. *Abnormal Psychology.* 2nd ed. New York: W. W. Norton and Company.

Rothbaum, B. O., E. B. Foa, D. S. Riggs, T. Murdock, and W. Walsh. 1992. A prospective examination of post-traumatic stress disorder in rape victims. *Journal of Traumatic Stress* 3:455–475.

Rothbaum, B. O., and L. F. Hodges. 1999. The use of virtual reality exposure in the treatment of the anxiety disorders. *Behavior Modification* 23:507–526.

Seligman, M. E. 1974. Depression and learned helplessness. In *The Psychology of Depression: Contemporary Theory and Research.* Edited by R. J. Friedman and M. M. Katz. Washington, D.C.: Winston.

Selye, H. 1956. *The Stress of Life.* New York: McGraw-Hill.

Smith, T. W., J. D. Sanders, and J. F. Alexander. 1990. What does the Cook and Medley Hostility Scale measure? Affect, behavior, and attributions in the marital context. *Journal of Personality and Social Psychology* 58:699–708.

Tomaka, J., R. Palacios, K. T. Schneider, M. Colotla, J. B. Concha, and M. M. Herrald. 1999. Assertiveness predicts threat and challenge reactions to potential stress among women. *Journal of Personality and Social Psychology* 76:1008–1021.

Tremayne, K., and E. S. Kubany. 1998. Differential prevalence and impact of intimate partner abuse among women and men in a substance abuse program. Poster presented at the Annual Convention of the American Psychological Association in San Francisco.

Williams, L. M. 1994. Recall of childhood trauma: A prospective study of women's memories of childhood sexual abuse. *Journal of Consulting and Clinical Psychology* 62(6):1167–1176.

Some Other
New Harbinger Titles

The End of-life Handbook, Item 5112 $15.95

The Mindfulness and Acceptance Workbook for Anxiety, Item 4993 $21.95

A Cancer Patient's Guide to Overcoming Depression and Anxiety, Item 5044 $19.95

Handbook of Clinical Psychopharmacology for Therapists, 5th edition, Item 5358 $55.95

Disarming the Narcissist, Item 5198 $14.95

The ABCs of Human Behavior, Item 5389 $49.95

Rage, Item 4627 $14.95

10 Simple Solutions to Chronic Pain, Item 4825 $12.95

The Estrogen-Depression Connection, Item 4832 $16.95

Helping Your Socially Vulnerable Child, Item 4580 $15.95

Life Planning for Adults with Developmental Disabilities, Item 4511 $19.95

Overcoming Fear of Heights, Item 4566 $14.95

*Acceptance & Commitment Therapy for the Treatment of Post-Traumatic Stress Disorder &
    Trauma-Related Problems*, Item 4726 $58.95

But I Didn't Mean That!, Item 4887 $14.95

Calming Your Anxious Mind, 2nd edition, Item 4870 $14.95

10 Simple Solutions for Building Self-Esteem, Item 4955 $12.95

The Dialectical Behavior Therapy Skills Workbook, Item 5136 $21.95

The Family Intervention Guide to Mental Illness, Item 5068 $17.95

Finding Life Beyond Trauma, Item 4979 $19.95

Five Good Minutes at Work, Item 4900 $14.95

It's So Hard to Love You, Item 4962 $14.95

Energy Tapping for Trauma, Item 5013 $17.95

Thoughts & Feelings, 3rd edition, Item 5105 $19.95

Transforming Depression, Item 4917 $12.95

Helping A Child with Nonverbal Learning Disorder, 2nd edition, Item 5266 $15.95

Leave Your Mind Behind, Item 5341 $14.95

Learning ACT, Item 4986 $44.95

ACT for Depression, Item 5099 $42.95

Integrative Treatment for Adult ADHD, Item 5211 $49.95

Freeing the Angry Mind, Item 4380 $14.95

Living Beyond Your Pain, Item 4097 $19.95

Transforming Anxiety, Item 4445 $12.95

Integrative Treatment for Borderline Personality Disorder, Item 4461 $24.95

Depressed and Anxious, Item 3635 $19.95

Is He Depressed or What?, Item 4240 $15.95

Cognitive Therapy for Obsessive-Compulsive Disorder, Item 4291 $39.95

Child and Adolescent Psychopharmacology Made Simple, Item 4356 $14.95

Call **toll free, 1-800-748-6273,** or log on to our online bookstore at **www.newharbinger.com** to order. Have your Visa or Mastercard number ready. Or send a check for the titles you want to New Harbinger Publications, Inc., 5674 Shattuck Ave., Oakland, CA 94609. Include $4.50 for the first book and 75¢ for each additional book, to cover shipping and handling. (California residents please include appropriate sales tax.) Allow two to five weeks for delivery.

Prices subject to change without notice.